LEMONADE TONIGHT

LEMONADE TONIGHT

Notes from a POW
and a Present-Day Journey of Discovery

Fiona Cameron & Carole Grant

Dot—
Hope you enjoy reading our story
as much as we enjoyed writing
it!
    With love,
        Carole & Fiona

9th July 2021

DEDICATION

for

Allan, Laura, Faye and Lauren.

In memory of your grandfather, Allan Cameron

Contents

Illustrations

INTRODUCTION

Our father, Allan Cameron, like many survivors of the second world war, rarely spoke about the past. For the most part, he put memories of his war experiences aside and looked to the future. Only very occasionally and when least expected, Dad would recall a wartime memory. Sadly, at the time we thought little about it. Today, we would have so many questions.

In June 1940 our father was taken prisoner at St Valery-en-Caux in France along with thousands of others from the 51st Highland Division and marched into captivity. Two weeks earlier the remarkable and successful Dunkirk evacuation had begun and what happened to those who were left behind fighting under French command in the Battle of France is sadly often regarded as a footnote in Scottish military history.

We remained in the dark about those early days in 1940 but when we made a chance discovery amongst our late father's papers many years later, it sparked our interest, and we were keen to find out more. Although compiling a book had never been our initial intention, we were encouraged by friends and family to put pen to paper. What was intended to be a simple account of our father's wartime experiences, inspired by his writings, turned out to be much more as a curious series of twists and turns began to link the past to the present with unexpected and heart-warming results.

Writing *Lemonade Tonight* was a challenge we embraced as we became more engrossed and involved. As inexperienced co-writers we spent many hours together, fuelled by endless cups of tea, sharing the research, writing and editing between us.

The account of our father's wartime experiences evolved into a story enriched by people, places and events that Dad, his close wartime friends and many others from the 51st Highland Division had shared. As many from our generation grew up knowing little about their relative's military involvement in this crucial episode from WW2, we feel it is a piece of history that deserves to be remembered.

Dear Dad,

Although you are not able to read the words we have written down we hope that, had you been able to, you would consider that we managed to give a true and fair account of your personal experiences and that you would be happy for your story to be told in this way. Using your own words made the most sense we thought, so as much as possible this is exactly what we have tried to do.

We know that you would have been every bit as surprised and pleased as we were with everything that unfolded. There were many times when we paused to imagine your reaction when something new came to light! So often we wished you were there to share the moment – you were never far from our thoughts.

Carole and Fiona

One

Looking Back

September 2011

There were three small notebooks. Each one was different, but they all had dark blue covers and looked as though they belonged together. A slight fusty smell still lingered over them. We were curious.

As we carefully flicked through the fragile pages there was no doubt that the cramped handwriting was our father's, but it was what was written that took us by surprise. They were not just everyday notebooks. The dates and entries showed that they were unmistakably diaries from the Second World War.

We had come across the notebooks randomly scattered at the bottom of an old, battered, brown suitcase underneath a collection of assorted and long forgotten war memorabilia that had belonged to our late father. The suitcase had been given to us by our stepmother, Dorothy, after our father passed away and we became its keepers. 'He went through a lot you know...' she said as she handed it over but at that time it was too soon for us to ask questions or to want to know more about the past. Apart from a few items once loaned to a local exhibition, the case was unceremoniously stored in the back of the garage where it lay untouched for another eighteen years.

Having now found our Dad's war diaries, it seemed an ideal

opportunity to discover more about a time in his life about which we knew little. His personal archives had lain untouched for seven decades and sadly age had taken its toll. We were keen to start reading his 'pennings', but we could see that before long the smudged and faded writing would be illegible. Making a transcript seemed the only way to preserve the fragile contents and, as it happened, the timing of our discovery could not have been better.

Two years before, Carole's diagnosis of the same cancer that had suddenly and tragically taken our mother's life forty years ago was a shock. It took eighteen months of treatment and the support of medical staff, family, friends and Maggie's Highlands to move forward. With renewed faith and fresh priorities, a new focus was welcome. We had no idea then that transcribing Dad's diaries would turn out to be much more than just a short-term distraction.

Our father rarely spoke about the war and it was not a subject that was ever talked about at home. It was only years later that we learned from his sister Jean that she too knew little about what he had witnessed or experienced. On the odd occasion when Dad did mention his wartime memories, we were too young or too preoccupied with our own thoughts to pay much attention. We were unaware of the significance of what was being said and there may have been stories that we heard but have now forgotten. It never occurred to us to write anything down and we always sensed not to ask questions. Occasionally we would hear comments about the lack of food and how difficult it was to keep warm during the bitter winter temperatures but even when the odd German word slipped into the conversation, we thought little of it. By the time we were adults the war was history.

From what little we had heard, we knew that Dad had been in the army, spent time in France and at some point, had been a prisoner of war in German-occupied Poland. The majority of young men from the Highlands who were called up in 1939 joined the Seaforth or Cameron Highlanders but there was nothing we had ever seen or heard to suggest that our father had been part of one of those well-known infantry regiments. We had no idea what part he had played in the war but what we did know for certain was that the time he spent in France had left a lasting impression.

Dad had warm memories of the generosity and bravery of the civilian population and loved all things French. He had a fondness for the language, the people, the food and the climate. French Beaujolais, he always said, was 'the best in the world.' After the war France was his favourite holiday destination. A family seaside trip to St Malo and Dinard in the 1950s was soon followed by a visit to Paris. A few years later we journeyed to the south of France sadly unaware that our stay in Menton would be our last family holiday together.

With his dark, deep-set eyes, heavy eyebrows and black wavy hair we imagined our father had a passing resemblance to the actor John Le Mesurier. Clothes sat well on his tall frame and he liked to dress smartly and buy the best that he could afford. 'A good-looking man suits anything,' he would jokingly say. Dad had a slim build but when he returned to the UK, he had been concerned enough about his persistent low weight to seek medical advice. All was well, but he had a small appetite, and many foods did not agree with him. Perhaps, like many others who returned from the prison camps, the years of meagre rations and a poor diet had taken its toll.

As hunger was a constant companion for those in captivity, regular parcels from the Red Cross were a lifeline for British POWs. Our father often remarked how indebted and grateful he was to all those who had been involved in improving their conditions in the camps. His sister Milly became a committed Red Cross volunteer and during her lifetime continued to give her time freely to raise funds and support their cause.

Throughout the turbulent years in Northern Europe, it was close ties between fellow comrades that were to help many get through uncertain times. For some those friendships were never forgotten and many, like our father's, were to endure a lifetime. While living in Glasgow in the 1950s and early 1960s we met two of our father's 'army friends' and their families many times over the years, and it was those frequent visits that gave us some of our most lasting early childhood memories.

Dad was the proud user of a company car and enjoyed taking us out for a drive when the opportunity arose. At weekends we would regularly travel across the city from our home in Knightswood to visit his wartime friends - Alistair MacRitchie or Johnnie McComiskey. They were both married, and each had two sons. At the McComiskey's house we remember playing board games or venturing outside if the weather was fine while the adults talked and perhaps occasionally reminisced about the war. Afterwards we joined the grown-ups for tea and biscuits, and it was those warm, cosy times when everyone was together chatting and laughing which are among our favourite memories of those visits.

There was also one other 'army pal' of Dad's, whom he regularly spoke about, called Archie Dey. Although we never met Archie and have no recollection of our father ever visiting him, it was a name that we knew well. 'I wonder what Archie Dey's up to?' Dad would often ask. There was never an answer to his question, but Mum would occasionally remark, 'I've really no idea Allan...'. Although we knew that Alistair, Archie and Johnnie were wartime pals of our father's, we had no idea or inkling as to how they met or knew our Dad.

In the early 1960s we left Glasgow to live in the North East of Scotland when we were aged only ten and three. Dad still kept in touch with Johnnie and his friendship with Alistair remained as close as ever. Despite the distance, we can recall occasional visits were made by both Johnnie and Alistair up until the late 1960s.

Having moved to a small seaside town it was a treat for us to spend family time at the beach and the Links during the summer months where we spent many happy hours with our father playing putting or learning how to master table tennis 'top spins'. Quiet pastimes seemed to suit Dad's nature and during the winter evenings he would happily spend hours patiently teaching us card games such as whist, rummy or cribbage. But it was bridge that was his real passion.

Thursday night at the local Bridge Club was rarely missed and a bridge 'foursome' at our house was a familiar routine. The card table and deck of cards were set out with precision and we were primed to serve tea and sandwiches at nine o'clock - on the dot. Over the years Dad's regular bridge partners, John Boyd, Johnny Gaul and David

Stewart became firm friends. David had been a World War Two POW in the Far East and in later years we learned that he and Dad often spoke together about their experiences.

Lochindorb is a picturesque freshwater loch in the Highlands and in the late 1960s our father enjoyed spending summer evenings at the lochside. He would look out his rods, pack his old army shoulder bag with tackle and take Fiona on a fishing trip! Occasionally, other pieces of assorted army gear would be unearthed from the garage. Once a tattered army drawstring kit bag was put to good use for a weekend Girl Guide camp.

Our Mum was outgoing, sociable, full of energy and life. Her unexpected illness and early death in 1970, when she was only fifty years old, was a shock and a devastating blow to all of us. After eighteen years of marriage our father was left widowed with two daughters amidst ongoing plans to emigrate to Australia.

Family life changed forever, and the emptiness was in some way filled by a closeness and unspoken understanding between the three of us. Our plans to emigrate were never mentioned again and in the months that followed Dad became quieter and more introspective. 'Loneliness is a terrible thing,' he once said.

We grew up knowing that the church had always been a part of our father's life and as a family we remember regularly attending the Church of Scotland. As a child Dad had gone to a Wesleyan Sunday School and after Mum died Dad gained comfort from Methodist Church services and occasionally, we would join him. Although he never spoke about what faith or religion meant to him our father showed by example and when we were in our twenties, he gave us both copies of *The Good News Bible* with a short handwritten inscription.

As time went on, Dad spoke less about the past, so we were taken aback when, on separate occasions, he mentioned two harrowing incidents which he had witnessed during the war. Both times we were busy in the kitchen setting the table or clearing up when these fragments from Dad's memory unexpectedly slipped into the conversation. It was as if his thoughts had transported him to another

11

time and place.

Once we heard a graphic account of how he and others had tried to help seriously injured soldiers who were in a desperate life or death situation. We could see he was deeply affected by what he had seen and troubled by how little he felt he could do. As we were growing up, he would often say to us 'You can only do your best,' and perhaps that was what he told himself that day when he knew that even his best would never be enough.

On another occasion we heard a description of the horrendous conditions that many thousands of starving Russian prisoners of war had to endure. He was clearly haunted by the memory of what he had known was happening. These incidents were never spoken about again and perhaps we should have seized the opportunity to ask questions ... but we never did. Yet the memory of what he told us remains vividly in our minds.

It is difficult to say what long term effects the war had on Dad. He had a strong inner resilience although there were times when he became quiet and withdrawn and we sensed that his thoughts were again in the past, but for the most part he remained positive, looked with optimism to the future and kept himself busy with work and his favourite hobbies. Dad was also unswervingly loyal towards close friends and family and perhaps this was a quality he had grown to appreciate during his time as a young man in the army. He had an ability to resolve any crisis or upset calmly and without judgement and people who met him often said he was a true gentleman. We had to agree. Although not demonstrative by nature, Dad made sure that we knew he was there for us and we never once doubted his love or his concern for our welfare. Home would always be there no matter what the future held.

At weekends there were few things Dad enjoyed more than watching WW2 films. Fiona and I would join Dad in front of the television to view such classics as *The Colditz Story* and *The Wooden Horse*. We were thrilled by those dramatised versions of life behind barbed wire and enthralled by the heroic adventures portrayed on screen, but although Dad watched intently, he never passed comment even though it must have brought back many memories. It was hard for us to believe that he too had spent years as a prisoner of war.

From his POW experiences our father knew only too well how important it was to hear news from home. He put this into practice and when we were students, he regularly sent us copies of the local newspaper. Once a 'Red Cross' parcel containing Vitamin C tablets arrived through the post complete with detailed handwritten advice and instructions on how to avoid winter coughs and colds!

Sadly, our father's own health was never robust and for as long as we can remember he suffered frequent chest infections. He gave up cigarettes, smoked a pipe and had an occasional cigar instead. It was not until he was in his sixties that he finally gave up smoking altogether. Spells of alarming night sweats which, once malaria was ruled out, remained unexplained.

Not once did Dad ever express any outward sign of regret or bitterness about what had happened during and after the war and we feel fortunate to have grown up in a family atmosphere free of prejudice and judgement. By the time our father was in his mid-sixties we thought his memories of the war had faded until one day a square self-addressed cardboard box appeared on the kitchen table.

Unknown to us, in 1984 he had applied to the Ministry of Defence for his war medals and, as with most armed forces personnel during the conflict, he was eligible for two awards. One was the 1939-45 Star Medal awarded to subjects of the British Commonwealth. The second one was the War Medal 1939-45 which was given to those who had served in the armed services for at least twenty-eight days.

Each year without comment or fuss, Dad would pin those medals to his jacket and join the local armistice parade when health and weather allowed. He never expressed his feelings, but he seemed proud to be part of the occasion and to take his place alongside others as they marched to the War Memorial. It was the only public acknowledgement of his army connections that we ever witnessed. Only a few years after receiving recognition of his wartime service our father unexpectedly and suddenly passed away.

At the outbreak of World War Two, Dad, along with thousands of others, was preparing to embark on an uncertain future and now exactly seventy-two years later we were on the brink of uncovering his story through his newly discovered diaries.

This is his story and ours.

Two

Early Life in Inverness

1918 to October 1939

At 10.15 in the evening, in a small mid-Victorian house in Lower Kessock Street, Inverness, our father Allan, the only son of Amelia Forbes Allan and William Cameron, was born. The date was Friday 18 October 1918, and World War One had entered its fifth year. Barely a month later the guns fell silent, ending the hostilities. There were celebrations across the country and the *Inverness Courier*, published on 12 November 1918, reported that bells rang out across the town while cheering crowds filled the streets and the local pipe band played to add to the celebratory atmosphere.[1]

At that time the Cameron family lived in a traditionally working-class area called Merkinch, one of the oldest parts of the burgh of Inverness. 34 Lower Kessock Street, as well as most of the other houses on that road, have long since been demolished and new low-rise apartment blocks have taken their place. Merkinch is close to the harbour area and nearby was the ferry linking North and South Kessock, a service which was replaced in 1982 by a bridge across the Moray Firth.

Dad had two older sisters, Amelia and Jane, known to the family as Milly and Jean. Before World War One their father William had

1. William & Amelia Cameron, circa 1914.

worked as an iron moulder at Rose Street Foundry and Engineering Company (later to become AI Welders), a prominent local employer at that time. Although the former foundry head office building on Academy Street still remains, the workshops themselves were mostly demolished or altered many years ago.

When World War One was declared on 4 August 1914, our grandfather William was just twenty-four years of age. The following month he joined the Inverness-shire Royal Horse Artillery Regiment, 1/1st Battery, as a gunner.[2] At that time the Regiment's HQ was in Margaret Street, Farraline Park, Inverness, although the original drill hall now forms part of a community meeting space. By early 1916 William's unit had joined the Egyptian Expeditionary Force, operating alongside an Anzac Mounted Division in Alexandria. During the time he served in Egypt William undertook further military training and in November 1916 qualified as a 1st Class Signaller. The following year he was promoted to Bombardier. Unfortunately, William became unwell shortly after this promotion and was admitted to the Field Hospital before being invalided back to England on 29 August 1917 on the Glasgow built Canadian hospital ship *HMHS Llandovery Castle*.[3]

Shortly after his return home in October 1917, William was discharged from the army due to being physically unfit for war service. Sadly, his health continued to deteriorate, and he died on 22 June 1923 aged just 33 years. Dad was only four years old at this time. William's death certificate lists lymphadenoma (malignant lymphoma) as the cause of death although family stories allude to a mystery illness contracted whilst overseas.

Widowed in her late twenties, our grandmother Amelia never remarried but was determined to work hard to provide for her young family. She took pride in always buying the best that she could afford for her children and they were always well turned out. However, she was grateful for and appreciated the parcels of 'good clothes' for the family sent over from the USA by her sister Meg.

It was towards the end of the war when Meg, aged just twenty, met an American sailor called Clyde Solt. During 1918, over 1000

American naval personnel arrived in Inverness and the US Naval Base 18 was formed. In an effort to deter German U-boats from reaching the North Atlantic using the route around the north of Scotland, the US Navy and The Royal Navy planned the creation of a huge minefield in the North Sea. This two hundred and thirty-mile-long 'Northern Barrage' stretched between Orkney and Norway and eventually used over seventy thousand sea mines.[4]

Clyde Solt arrived in Inverness aboard the USS *Black Hawk* as a Chief Radio Electrician and was stationed at US Naval Base 18. As Merkinch was adjacent to the Inverness harbour area and the naval base, US sailors could occasionally be seen making their way up Lower Kessock Street towards the town centre. After a whirlwind romance, Meg and Clyde were married in Inverness on 7 April 1919 and later that same year they made the long sea journey across the Atlantic to begin their new life together in the USA. We still maintain close links with Meg's granddaughter and great-grandchildren in the United States.

In the early 1930s the Cameron family moved closer to Inverness town centre and into a large house in Huntly Place. Amelia and her children lived here for about five years before eventually making Dochfour Drive their home in 1937, when Dad was nineteen years old.

As a young boy our father attended Merkinch Public School and we still have a number of books he was awarded during his younger years. Some were for perfect attendance for as much as five years, whilst others were prizes for classwork. The impression we have is of a conscientious and studious boy who worked hard at school and took his education very seriously.

He was a keen member of the 6th Inverness Company Boys Brigade and had fond memories about his camping expeditions near Inverness which seemed largely to feature fields, bell tents and bicycles. In 1931, aged about thirteen, he was awarded the 'Boys Brigade Certificate in Ambulance and First Aid to the injured' – knowledge which, unknown to him at the time, he was going to find useful in later years.

Sunday School was also a regular part of his early life and he carefully kept a collection of books received as prizes from the Inverness Wesleyan Methodist Sunday School during the mid 1920s. Again, some were for perfect attendance whilst others were for his diligence.

Dad was a bright pupil and after leaving primary school he was one of only two or three young people in the Inverness and Islands area to win a £9 bursary to attend the Inverness Royal Academy. This bursary was worth about £490 in 1930 and was not an insubstantial sum! It meant the family did not have to pay school fees although they still had to cover the cost of books, jotters and other necessities. He did well at the Academy and came away with a leaving certificate which included Higher French, Lower German and Latin. He was not to know how relevant these language skills were to be in just a few years' time.

When his school days were over our father decided to follow a career in the legal profession. He began studying to be a solicitor and in June 1938 was indentured as a law apprentice to George Ross and Noble, Solicitors, Inverness for a period of five years. At that time, entering into the profession meant a further three years at university to obtain a Bachelor of Law degree. Many years later we learned from his sister Jean that Dad had planned to study at either Glasgow or Edinburgh University. Dad was only in his second year of training when on 3 September 1939, a wireless broadcast by Prime Minister Neville Chamberlain announced that a state of war existed between Britain and Germany. Later that same day King George VI addressed his people, both at home and overseas.

> 'For the second time in the lives of most of us, we are at war. Over and over again we have tried to find a peaceful way out of the differences between ourselves and those who are now our enemies. But it has been in vain.' [5]

Our father received his call up papers when he was in hospital for a minor operation – the date was 18 October 1939, his twenty-first birthday. Earlier that morning the official brown envelope had arrived through the letterbox at Dochfour Drive and was brought to the hospital by his anxious mother when she visited later that day. On reading the letter Dad realised that he only had a couple of weeks in which to recover from his operation and prepare himself for not only leaving home but also giving up his hard-earned position at the solicitors' office in Inverness.

On Wednesday 1 November, Dad said goodbye to his mother and sister Jean before boarding the train at Inverness railway station to travel to Aberdeen, some one hundred and eight miles away. At that time, he had no idea when he would next see his family, but we are sure none of them imagined it would be almost four long years before he would at last be home. Having already lost her husband soon after his return from the First World War, we can only imagine with how heavy a heart Amelia said goodbye to her only son as he set off from the station that day.

Hours after war was declared, Britain used the RAF to drop more than six thousand aerial propaganda pamphlets over German territories in an effort to try and convince the ordinary German people that confrontation could still be avoided. Addressed to 'German Men and Women' the leaflet said:

> 'The Government of the Reich have, with cold deliberation, forced war upon Great Britain. They have done so knowing that it must involve mankind in a calamity worse than that of 1914.'[6]

It continued by saying that Britain desired peace and that the German people could also insist on stopping the war at any time. It declared that Britain was ready to negotiate with the German government if they also wished for peace.

As Dad left Inverness, he may still have had some hope that the newly declared war would all be over quickly and that he would be back home in just a few months. It was a time of fear and great uncertainty for everyone.

Three

A Memoir

October to Early December 2011

Now that we had found our father's wartime diaries, we wasted no time in beginning to transcribe his first notebook. It was a promising start as on the first page Dad had listed details of the army unit he had been attached to, including his service number. With this information we were now able to begin to research and find out details about the well-known 51st Division that our father had been part of.

Surprisingly, it did not take long to begin to accumulate a sizeable amount of war-related resources. Military books were recommended, and some were generously loaned to us by others interested in the history of World War Two. The internet also gave us a wealth of information and quickly became a valued resource. Soon the spare room was littered with maps of Northern Europe, assorted books about World War Two and the 51st HD. Before long it was beginning to resemble the 'War Office'.

By now it was early November and, on the run-up to Armistice Sunday, there was an increase in media coverage relating to past wars. One morning we heard an interesting Radio Scotland report that featured the memoirs of a local war veteran who had been in the 51st Highland Division in 1940 like our father. We wrote down brief details and made a mental note to explore at a later date more about the history of veterans who had served in the army at this time.

There was plenty of useful information about the 51st to sift through but finding specific details about our father's unit proved difficult although our search did lead us to a website link dedicated to helping relatives to trace family members who had been in the conflict. Using army details from our father's diary we entered his name before extending the search to include the names of his wartime friends, Archie Dey and Johnnie McComiskey. When this was unsuccessful, we made a final attempt using Alistair MacRitchie's name.

The results showed only one war-related item half-way down the first page. The name of a book was displayed and the word 'Lager' in the title and the name 'Stuart MacRitchie,' immediately caught our attention. Knowing that 'Lager' was a German word for camp and

2. Allan Cameron, Archie Dey, Alistair
MacRitchie 'The Three Musketeers'.

having a hunch that Stuart might well be the name of Alistair's younger son, we wasted no time in heading straight to the book preview.

The publication had been compiled by Stuart with the help of his brother George and was called *Christmas in the Lager - Worse than a Sunday*. It contained the war memoirs of an Alistair MacRitchie who was their late father. A scan through the first few pages of the preview showed that the information tied in closely to what we knew so far about our own father's experiences. Background information about Alistair's profession as an architect to his roots in Fort William matched what we could remember from the past and a photograph of a young man in army uniform looked very much like the Alistair we had known. We felt sure it was Dad's close friend from his army days but it was the discovery of a second photograph that confirmed our suspicions.

The full-page image was of three men in army uniform with a caption that read,

Allan Cameron, Archie Dey, Alistair MacRitchie 'The Three Musketeers' or 'The Three Must Get Beers'

We recognised the photograph immediately as there was an identical print, without names, in our father's collection. There were no notes relating to the origin or date of Alistair's photograph but now that we could identify Archie Dey we were able to recognise him in other wartime snapshots belonging to our father. Where the three men had first met we still had no idea but it seemed they were good pals and enjoyed each other's company!

For us it was an astonishing and extraordinary piece of good luck to have discovered Alistair's memoirs. We were delighted at such an unexpected and positive outcome from a chance internet search! As we again looked through the book preview for details that we may have missed it was a pencil sketch on the front cover that caught our attention. At first glance it appeared to be an artist's interpretation of a typical war scene, but to us it seemed oddly familiar. The drawing of ambulances and men lying in a ditch reminded us of the tragic event Dad had once vividly described. It may well have been a coincidence, but we were now curious to try and find out more if we could.

Our thoughts turned to our father and to what he may have felt about our discovery of Alistair's memoirs had he been here. No doubt he would have been astonished and delighted, in his own understated way, to hear the news. 'Alistair's memoirs? Fancy that...' We were sure he would also have been amazed at the power of technology that had enabled us to find Alistair's book within minutes.

In the post-war years we had met Alistair and his wife Helen on many occasions. Even after Dad and Alistair had died, we kept in touch with Helen. It was only after she passed away that all links with the MacRitchie family ended, until now.

It was only by an extraordinary stroke of good luck and fortuitous timing that our discovery of Dad's diaries and the publication of *Christmas in the Lager – worse than a Sunday* had coincided. The book had only been compiled in 2010 and recently made available on the internet. If we had searched just a few months previously there would have been no book to find. We may have come across it at some future date but the outcome of what eventually transpired would have been very different. Now all we had to do was order two copies of the publication ... from abroad.

Details on the website explained that Stuart lived in Vancouver and that copies of his book could be ordered from an online publishing company. Placing an order was straightforward but we were also keen to message Stuart and George to let them know that we had come across their fathers' memoirs and to explain that we were Allan Cameron's daughters.

Contacting Stuart directly was not possible but, on the advice of the publishing company, we left a brief message on the recommended social media site, satisfied that an automatic alert would arrive in his in-box.

Two weeks later in early December, we were delighted when two grey hardback copies of *Christmas in the Lager - Worse than a Sunday* arrived through the post, but we had not yet heard back from Stuart.

Four

Leaving Home

November 1939 to May 1940

When the Inverness train finally pulled into Aberdeen our father immediately made his way to join the other new recruits at the Gordon Barracks near Bridge of Don. It was here on 1 November 1939, that he was enlisted in the 153rd Highland Field Ambulance (153 FA)[1] as a member of the RAMC (Royal Army Medical Corps), and part of the 51st Highland Division (51st HD). The Royal Army Medical Corps is a specialist corps in the British Army which provides medical services to all British Army personnel and their families in war and peace. Because it is not a fighting arm (non-combatant), under the Geneva Conventions, members of the RAMC are protected. During World War Two they were entitled to wear red cross armbands and also to display the emblem on their vehicles. [2]

His record of service paper shows that he was 'deemed to have been enlisted into the Territorial Army for the duration of the emergency under the provisions of The National Service (Armed Forces) Act 1939'. From *Christmas in the Lager – Worse than a Sunday* we discovered that Alistair also enlisted in Aberdeen on the same day as our father. To our surprise we found that their army numbers were only six digits apart and perhaps it was here, at the very start of their army lives, that their long-standing friendship had begun. We later found out that Archie Dey, the 'Third Musketeer', had also been told to report to Aberdeen on 1 November.

As Dad signed his army registration papers that day, he was not to know that he was destined to be part of one of the most significant events in the history of the 51st HD and that it would be many years before those who survived would see home again.

The 51st HD, first formed in 1908, already had a reputation for being an outstanding infantry division following their participation in World War One. In 1939, the Division was again mobilised as part of the BEF for deployment to France, commanded by Major General V. M. Fortune, C.B., D.S.O. It comprised nine infantry battalions formed into three brigades – 152nd, 153rd and 154th. The five Highland Regiments provided the men – the Black Watch, The Seaforth Highlanders, The Queen's Own Cameron Highlanders, The Gordon Highlanders and the Argyll & Sutherland Highlanders. In January 1940 when they left for France, there were three RAMC Field Ambulances under command of ADMS, Lt. Col. D. P. Levack – the 152 FA, 153 FA and 154 FA.[3]

In 1938 the 153 FA was formed in anticipation of increased hostilities in Europe and on 1 September 1939 at its Woolmanhill, Aberdeen depot, it received the official telegram to mobilise. On 4 September General Officer Commanding of the 51st Highland Division, Major General Fortune, visited the unit and a month later on 9 October the 153 FA travelled to Morval Barracks, Farnborough by special train. After the unit had left, the nearby Gordon Barracks base at Bridge of Don was used for registration of new RAMC recruits, like our father, from all over Scotland.

The registration process at Bridge of Don did not take long and later that very same evening the newly enlisted men, including our father, all still dressed in their civilian clothes, boarded a train to take them on the long journey south from Aberdeen to Hampshire, England. Almost twenty-four hours later they arrived at Morval Barracks, Farnborough to join the main body of the 153 FA, increasing their total of other ranks to around 220. About a month later the unit moved to Boyce Barracks (previously known as Haig Lines) near

Crookham, which was at that time the base training depot for the RAMC.

Instruction for the recruits, completed during November and December, was intense and included route marches, battle physical training and drill, night-time exercises, practice in concealment, taking cover, camouflage and defence against gas. The following extract on treating gas poisoning was found in Dad's handwritten notes:

> 'Lewisite is similar – colourless in pure state – no smell off vapour – remains a liquid in low temp. – less persistent than mustard gas but quicker in penetration. Penetrates skin immediately, rubber etc in half time of mustard gas – heavy oily fabrics are good protection, but gas destroys the oil film – wet clothing has increased resistance. It is destroyed by water – contains arsenic! Dangerous to drink contaminated water. Pain & irritation on skin after contact with gas – contaminated food causes arsenic poison – blisters form quickly – skin red in 15 mins – blisters 1-4 hours – may be fatal.'

Instruction on stretcher bearing was also an important part of the programme as were lectures on, for example, first aid, bandaging, treatment of wounds and dealing with shock.

Uniforms were also issued during this time and below is a list we found among Dad's papers:

SIZE	ROLLS
Garment	*Size*
GREATCOAT, D.S.	7
JACKET OR BLOUSE	8
TROUSERS, S.D. or B.D.	13
DENIM TROUSERS	13
SHIRT, ANGORA	5
VESTS, WOOLLEN	3
DRAWERS, WOOLLEN	3
DRAWERS, CELLULAR	3
JERSEY, PULLOVER	2

JERKINS, LEATHER	2
SOCKS, WORSTED	2
BOOTS, ANKLE	8M
CAPS, F.S.A.R.	$6\,^7/_8$
HELMETS, U.K.	$6\,^7/_8$

Shortly after arrival, RAMC Training Manuals were issued for reference, ten copies to each barrack room. On 25 November, after just three weeks of instruction, the new recruits were given a test examination in first aid and practical bandaging and by the end of November they had all been allocated to one of the three companies of 153 FA (A, B & HQ). On completion of this concentrated period of instruction Dad could call himself a Nursing Orderly!

According to his Army Service Records, our Dad was graded and mustered as a Nursing Orderly Class III about three months later on 1 May 1940. Once you had gained sufficient experience it was possible to progress to Nursing Orderly Second Class and then First Class. Unfortunately, Dad did not get this opportunity.

We can recall his sister - our aunt Jean - telling us that Dad had been earmarked for officer training in the early days of his army career along with one or two of his friends. They had been told they would have to complete duty overseas first, but circumstances determined that for our father the opportunity for promotion never arose.

Within just three months of his arrival at Crookham, Dad was due to be sent overseas to France on active duty.

He began writing in his first diary during January 1940 just before he left England. His initial entries are details of mail he received before his departure.

Got 5 letters on January 10th and eleven letters on January 20th

Got parcel of books on January 19th

Got 5 letters from mother and one from Arthur on January 27th

2 letters and Christmas card on 25th

A Christmas card reached him a month late and bundles of up to eleven letters arrived at one time so there was clearly some delay in mail reaching the new recruits. However, we soon discovered that Dad's mother Amelia was a very prolific letter writer and managed to maintain a regular flow of mail throughout the whole period he was away from home. Unfortunately, none of his or his mother's letters have survived.

Unit diaries indicate that embarcation leave was awarded to some of the men prior to leaving the UK although Dad makes no mention of this in his diary.

Overseas

In early January 1940, an advance party was dispatched to France and, although Dad was not a part of this group, he did leave later that same month. On the twenty-ninth, along with other members of the 153 FA, he travelled to Southampton docks by train. Here they boarded the *Ulster Monarch*, sleeping on board ship that night in readiness to sail for Le Havre at 7.30am the following morning. Our father was now part of the BEF (British Expeditionary Force). The BEF was created in February 1939 in response to the anticipation of hostilities with Germany and the first Divisions left for France soon after the outbreak of war in early September of that year. Their role was to support France in defending its borders in the event of an enemy attack.

Monday 29th January 1940
Left Crookham – Southampton. Slept on U Monarch,
cabins, heat – food

The *Ulster Monarch* was a passenger ship built by Harland and Wolff for the Belfast Steamship Company which normally provided regular sailings between Ireland and the UK. In October 1940 it was eventually requisitioned by the Admiralty and converted to a Landing

Ship Infantry (LSI).

Tuesday 30th January 1940

Sailed from Southampton at 7.30am - rough, sea sickness - arrived at Le Havre about 7pm -slept on Ulster Monarch

3. HMS Ulster Monarch LSI(H) 12 February 1944 ©Imperial War Museum (A 21806).Reproduced by kind permission of Imperial War Museum.

After a rough crossing with many men, including Dad, suffering from seasickness, they arrived at Le Havre docks and once more spent the night on board ship. On a wet and miserable last day of January the troops finally disembarked and were marched down to the local train station. Here they were forced to wait in the cold for some considerable time before finally making the thirty-mile journey to Yvetot. Within six months this small French town, capital of the Caux region in northern France, would be almost totally destroyed by the German Army.

Wednesday 31st January

Disembarked at Le Havre – rain. Food in station – marched to station for train (just about killed) – boarded train – left after 2 or 3 hours wait – arrived at Yvetot

Arrived in France – no food, heavy packs, rotten train journey – bullets – no light – cold, draughty

– went by lorry to Caudebec – slept in loft

From Yvetot a journey by lorry took them to Caudebec-en-Caux and it was here that they joined up with their advance party who had left the UK two or three weeks previously. Alistair MacRitchie had been a member of the advance party and we are sure it was here where our father once more met up with his friend.

Dad spent his first night on French soil sleeping in a loft – in the months that followed he would discover that the men were billeted in whatever space could be found for them and that very often it would be far from comfortable!

This was the time of the so-called Phoney War, the period up to May 1940 when there were almost no hostilities in Western Europe aside from minor clashes. The BEF were mainly engaged in digging defences on the Belgian-French border in anticipation of an attack. Poland however had already been occupied by the German Army following the invasion and German troops were making new plans to invade France through the Ardennes Forest, a move that would ultimately lead to France's surrender in June 1940.

It was likely that many of the young soldiers, newly arrived in France, had never been overseas before. During this spell of relative calm, when there was not always much for them to do, many seized the opportunity to enjoy the novelty of being in a different country, to meet local French citizens and to try their hand at speaking a foreign language.

Having studied French at school, Dad now had the chance to put his knowledge to practical use! His diary entry for the first day in France indicates that he had the opportunity to explore the local town and enjoy a break from army rations.

Thursday 1st February 1940
Went to Caudebec - speaking to the French inhabitants etc - visited cafes etc - food!!!

However, they were soon on the move again.

Saturday 3rd February 1940
Left Caudebec by lorry – arrived at Allery, billeted Hotel de la Sure – bully beef again!!

Although the hotel billet sounded grand, the reality was that these buildings were often disused or in disrepair and lacking in basic facilities such as running water, heat or light.

> *Allery – cold, no rations – no pay – waste of time –*
> *continual standing around – ridiculous work enforced on*
> *MO in Caudebec and Allery – latrines, roads etc etc…*

To keep the men occupied during these early weeks they were often ordered to repeatedly carry out drills for packing and unpacking the lorries, cleaning kit and so on. Dad seemed surprised when even the MO (Medical Officer) was made to carry out duties not normally part of his remit! The combination of bitterly cold weather, a lack of food and pay and a feeling that they had nothing useful to do was not what the men had expected. For the soldiers, occasional outings to the local estaminets provided some relief from the boredom, no doubt helped by the fact that alcohol was relatively cheap for the British servicemen!

Ten days later and they were once again on the move, this time to the village of Berguette which lies close to the town of Bethune and is within twenty-six miles of the city of Lille. On this occasion the local church hall provided accommodation but overall, the conditions were generally no better.

As the unit travelled gradually eastwards across northern France, in each place they stopped (Caudebec-en-Caux, Allery, Berguette) their billets were very basic, sometimes with no lights or heating. The men often had to sleep on bare, hard floors and conditions were draughty and extremely cold and uncomfortable. More often than not there was no running water or proper sanitation and the men had to dig their own latrines each time they moved to a new place. Frozen ground and freezing temperatures must have made this a very unpleasant and arduous task.

Monday 12th February 1940
Berguette – hard floor – no water – compulsory shaving
and kit and button polishing – full pay eventually – but
no cig issue – curiously enough there's plenty for sale! –
hospital – lack of sanitation etc

Tuesday 13th February 1940
Heavy snowfall - wash in snow!! Cold!

The months of January and February 1940 were the coldest recorded in Europe for forty-five years. On 13 February, when a diary entry mentions a heavy snowfall in Berguette, many other countries across Europe experienced bitterly cold weather and heavy snowstorms. The *Inverness Courier* reported on 30 January 1939 that:

'Home leave stopped for the BEF.

Severe weather conditions cause postponement.'[4]

On 2 February a further notice stated:

'Leave for the British Expeditionary Force is to be restored if the weather improves.'[5]

Wednesday 14th February 1940
Went down to Haillicourt for coal (mines of Bermony),
fire at pit-head – cold

Thursday 15th February 1940
Lorry picket – work at hospital

Friday 17th February 1940
(about 8 inches of snow) Back at hospital with MacRitchie
as NO's, [Nursing Orderlies] off at 2 – Enoch on – Dey &
M.R. gone to Bethune – lorry picket

As both Alistair MacRitchie and Archie Dey are mentioned on 17 February, we know that the three friends were together at this time.

Dad never gave any detail in his diaries about his RAMC Nursing Orderly duties, nor did he ever speak about this in later years but records from the time explain the role of the Field Ambulance during wartime.

According to the RAMC Training Manual of 1935, the Field Ambulance consisted of three companies – A, B and HQ. As noted in both Dad's diary and his service record he was part of HQ Company which held the more complex medical and surgical equipment and also formed the Main Dressing Station (MDS) which was usually situated some miles behind the ADS (Advanced Dressing Station). Field ambulance transport would collect casualties from the ADS and take them to the MDS which was capable of dealing with large numbers of sick and wounded. After assessment the most serious cases were then evacuated to the Casualty Clearing Station (CCS).[6]

During the time of the 'Phoney War' when there were few battle casualties to treat, the RAMC attended to everyday sicknesses and minor injuries and looked after the general health of the unit.

It is clear that Dad's diary entries from those early weeks in France focused more on the day-to-day practicalities of active service rather than on personal reflections. Army food rations, the price of local foodstuffs and calculations of the amount of money spent on essential items such as razor blades, matches and chocolate are listed in detail and we have a sense of the priorities important at that time. We know, for instance, that a 'writing pad, envelopes and pencil' cost the grand sum of seven francs.

> Choc for 10 francs
> Razor blades 3 – (10f)
> 4 Bars Choc (50f)
> 4 bars Choc 3f (10f)

We are sure our grandmother Amelia received letters from Dad during this time and must have looked forward expectantly to hearing from him and to know he was well.

Although Inverness in the Scottish Highlands was a relatively safe area during the war years, at home in Dochfour Drive in the early months of 1940, Amelia was nonetheless beginning to experience the hardships of wartime on the home front. Bacon, butter and sugar were rationed from 8 January with further ration schemes for meat, tea, jam, biscuits and other foods added later. Many fruits and vegetables became difficult to find. In the local newspapers she would have read about the introduction of ration books, the issue of gas masks, petrol rationing, and even notices for air raid warning siren tests. On 26 January 1940 the *Inverness Courier* printed a notice entitled *"Couriers" for Abroad*.

'Many readers of "The Courier" are in the habit of posting copies of the paper to friends in one or more of the countries listed below. The Defence Regulations forbid them to do so now.' [7]

It was now February and Dad had already spent three weeks in France.

The Move

Dad's diary showed that by 18 February 1940 he had been in the French town of Berguette for a week and during this time had been working in the hospital with Alistair as a Nursing Orderly. Unfortunately, pages from the diary have been torn out and there were no further entries until early May. We discovered however that Dad had also made a list of the towns and villages he had passed through, so we were able to begin mapping his journey and discovered that this route corresponded very closely to the known movements of the 51st HD during April, May and June 1940. We know that the unit spent time in Don Sainghin, Erquinghem-Leys and Armentières and continued to set up hospitals and carry out training drills as they had been doing since their arrival in France at the end of January.

Although diary entries provided no information for those few weeks from mid- February to early May, according to Alistair's recollections, he and Dad had some memorable times together with much merry-making! There was, for example, mention of a lady by the name of Suzanne– a mystery French woman whom our father had befriended in Erquinghem-Lys. There was also a night out in Lille which involved a ninety-franc taxi ride back to Don Sainghin! Stories of camaraderie frequently had a habit of starting with an over-indulgence of French hospitality and ending up with some near calamitous escapades on their way home! Visiting the local cafes for eggs, chips and beer was always popular although Alistair also speaks of the three of them becoming friendly with a local French family who generously invited them to their home for meals. Maybe it was around this time that Dad's fondness for all things French began.

However, things were about to change, as on 13 April 1940 Major General Fortune, who was in command of the 51st Highland Division, received word that his formation was to be detached from the rest of the BEF and moved almost 200 miles to the south-east. In the industrial Saar region, they would come under the command of the French 3rd Army as part of the Saar Force, which came into being on 1 May 1940. Around the middle of April, the Division left the Armentières area and over the course of three days travelled towards the town of Metz which was situated close to the Maginot Line and the border with Germany. The Maginot Line was an extensive series of fortifications built at great expense during the 1930s. It extended from the Swiss to the Franco-Belgian-Luxembourg borders and was intended to protect France's boundary with Germany. The Allies mistakenly believed it would provide a strong deterrent to the German Army and prevent any large-scale attack.[8]

As the Division travelled through the French countryside, their route took them close to places whose names were all too familiar, places where many of their own fathers and relatives had fought and even died during the First World War, just over twenty years before. It must have been very disheartening for all the men as they passed close to the sites of World War One battles and saw the many names inscribed on monuments. Although our grandfather William did not serve in France, Dad would still have been reminded of his father's service as a soldier. Throughout the journey, our father collected a number of postcards which he brought back home with him, some depicting memorials to the fallen of the Great War.

Using both Dad's list of towns and his postcard collection, we were able to trace his journey from when he arrived at Le Havre at the end of January until the Division reached the Saar in late April. (see route map on page 55).

In addition to supporting the French army, the Division's move provided an opportunity to carry out training and gain combat experience after the relative inactivity of the preceding weeks. Troops deployed in this region were about to be in direct contact with the enemy and it was here that the 51st HD had their first real taste of war.

Sometime towards the end of April and the beginning of May Dad was in Moyeuvre-Grande, a town lying close to the Belgian border, just to the north of Metz and known at that time for its iron ore mining industry. By the end of 1940 this town would fall under German rule and remain so until the end of the war in 1945.

Alistair wrote that they set up a small hospital here and were billeted in an old cinema. He also recalls 'nights out' with Allan and Archie so we know the friends were still all together.

There were very few entries in Dad's diary for the early part of May although we know from his service record that on 1 May he was graded and mustered as a Nursing Orderly Class III.

Five consecutive entries, from 5 to 9 May, consist entirely of lists of food which may have been army rations or more likely the contents of parcels from home. In any case, the items were varied!

Tuesday 7th May 1940
Pkt chewing gum, Pkt prunes, 2 pkts Yorkshire Pudding, 2 boxes cheese

Thursday 9th May 1940
2 Choc, peas, dates, tomato juice, Horlicks, salmon, Maltesers, figs, jam, margarine, 2pkts biscuits

May 10 was a significant day as this was when Winston Churchill became the new Prime Minster of Great Britain. It was also the day when Germany launched their invasion through the Low Countries and the Battle of France began. The German assault was so successful that they were able to push well into France within just five days and continue their advance at a very rapid rate. By 22 June France had signed an Armistice with Germany and hostilities between Germany, Italy and France ended on 25 June.

Although Dad has no diary entry for 10 May, he alluded to the

German invasion on 11 May with a brief note:

AIR RAID! (Ising Camp)

Ising is very close to Férange, which in turn is close to the Hackenberg Fort (Ouvrage Hackenberg), one of the fortifications that made up the Maginot Line.

The 'Phoney War' had come to an abrupt end for the BEF and they now found themselves engaged in full-scale hostilities.

Although the family at home in Inverness would have heard news of the German invasion, they probably had very little idea of Dad's whereabouts at this time and if he was anywhere near to the front lines. Detailed information was often withheld from newspaper articles. On 17 May 1940 an article appeared in the *Inverness Courier* about the war in Europe and it included the line:

> 'Details of the fighting are being withheld at present in the interest of the conduct of operations.' [9]

By 20 May Dad was in Charleville-sous-Bois, a small town just north-east of Metz. With the sudden increase in hostilities, the Field Ambulance was now seeing and treating an increasing number of battle casualties. Maybe because of the heightened tensions the men took their chance for relaxation whenever they could – a diary entry for 20 May was a brief note describing a great night out in the company of some French soldiers!

Charleville – French Sergeants Mess – G Room (Guard Room). Mac was terrific. Food!!!!!

Alistair recounts the same evening in a little more detail:

> 'Somewhere along the line in another chateau we were invited by a group of French NCO's to come for dinner. They were occupying a village nearby and were part of a unit who looked after the farm animals when the villages were evacuated. They did very well – meat and fowl on the hoof as it were. We ate several chickens as I recall,

enjoyed lively conversation and wine of the country. I recall standing up, looking at my watch aghast at the time, exclaiming 'we have to go' and, for some unknown reason, falling flat on my face! The NCO's took photos at our convivial evening, but I have never seen them and never will! We were transported back in a small van and dumped at the chateau gates. That was a night to remember, but the awakening in the guard room, with feet entangled in a bed spring, was also memorable in another respect. My two pals were on the floor. Maybe my stripe entitled me to the spring. We escaped being put on a charge as we were under 24 hours' notice to move.'[10]

Looking back, it is heartening that Dad's final diary entry for May marked an occasion he and his friends all enjoyed, as the course of their lives was soon to take a turn for the worse.

Five

Reflections

Mid December 2011

Dad had now been in France for almost four months as the 51st Division trailed across Northern France before heading south towards the Saar region. Using our Dad's lists of the towns he had stayed in, or passed through, as a starting point, we began to try and make sense of those early days. As we closely studied maps to trace his journey, it helped that his attention to detail ensured that every French place name was meticulously spelled.

There were many pages that had been torn out and diary entries were in note form. Abbreviations and Dad's unique brand of shorthand took time to decipher and transcribing was often a slow process as the pages were delicate. The writing was small and the entries written in pencil had become badly smudged after having become faded in storage. Often notes could only be read with the help of a bright light and strong magnifying glass. Nevertheless, we felt fortunate to have Dad's own record of the past as we later heard from a former comrade that keeping a diary during wartime conditions was not easy. He was also curious to know where Dad may have kept his notebooks hidden!

Researching and transcribing could be frustrating and time-consuming, but when even a small piece of personal or social history was uncovered it felt as though we had taken a giant step forward. References to transport and the movement of the 153 FA that we came across were helpful starting points as we tried to match our Dad's hastily written notes to well-documented historical facts. One of our early successes was when the notes led us to discover the full name, history and photograph of the ship *Ulster Monarch* that had taken him from Southampton to Le Havre in January 1940.

It was not just facts that were fascinating. From details of everyday life mentioned in Dad's notes we were inspired to imagine what it must have been like for him during those first few weeks in January as the troops travelled across the countryside of France and the winter started to bite.

The grey scenes which Dad hinted at in his diaries gradually turned to colour and became film-like. We could imagine the muffled sounds of heavy boots marching through deep snow while voices drifted from pit-head fires in Haillicourt. Never one to rush, we could picture Dad browsing in a local bureau de tabac calculating how many francs or centimes he could afford to spend. Perhaps he had time to write a letter home or roll a cigarette, or two, using the 'baccy' bought in Allery earlier that day, before curried mutton or 'bully beef' was served…yet again.

Amongst our father's post-war papers, we had recently come across two short, detailed and descriptive essays about Scotland that he had composed sometime after the war. Although Dad never wrote anything of length during his time in France, it was not hard to imagine that in the countryside and villages of France, Dad too may have allowed his thoughts and imagination to wander as he silently created images in words.

While writing up Dad's notes we still managed to find time to think about the past. We knew that our father had been in the Field Ambulance and had worked as a Nursing Orderly, yet it seemed strange that we had managed to coast through the rough and tumble of childhood injuries with no inkling that Dad had any knowledge of basic first aid, far less the skills to administer medical assistance on a battlefield! Our well-stocked medical box of various bandages and dressings might have been a clue to Dad's former training, but never once did he let it slip about his past.

Seeing our father's handwriting and reading his words gave a deep sense of connection and one afternoon while engrossed in his diaries, we had a strange and overwhelming feeling that he too was there with us.

Dad was just as we remembered him ... sitting on the easy chair, arms crossed, deep in thought. Although never daring to take a backward glance, we had a sense that he was at peace, content, and approved of our discovery of his wartime 'pennings'. Thoughts of these warm, reassuring and fleeting moments stayed with us in the weeks ahead as we tried to make sense of the past.

Our Dad's written words may have been the catalyst for these thoughts but as the present merged with the past, we understood the feelings of uncertainty, friendship, despair, hope and excitement which he would have known in those early days but not voiced. It seemed that recent events in our lives had made it possible for us to feel closer to him after all this time and we were sure that our Dad would not have been too surprised.

Once, when due to ill health, he was unable to travel to the funeral of his older sister Milly, he told us that, at the exact time of her cremation, he clearly heard her call out his name. What he experienced preyed on his mind and for days afterwards he spoke about how strange it felt. On another occasion we read in a letter that he and his wartime friend Alistair MacRitchie had once attended a spiritualist meeting in Glasgow. The idea of going to 'the Spooks!' as they called it, had come about after an evening at a classical recital. Whatever goings-on they witnessed at the meeting were never divulged.

Now that we had our own copies of Alistair MacRitchie's memoirs, *Christmas in the Lager – Worse than a Sunday*, it felt that we had gained a new and personal dimension to our Dad's story. Although Alistair's memoirs spanned the entire period of his involvement in the conflict, we initially focussed on the first six months and were surprised to discover that both men had been enlisted into the 153 FA on 1 November 1939 in Aberdeen before heading south to Hampshire. As we knew Dad had also trained at Crookham, Alistair's recollections of army training gave us a unique insight into what everyday experiences were really like for the young recruits. His humorous descriptions of their rudimentary accommodation, basic facilities and endless stretcher drills made entertaining reading!

By the time Alistair and Dad had been in France for a few weeks it was possible to compare Alistair's account with our Dad's diary entries and we were intrigued to discover instances when they had recorded similar information on the same dates. On one occasion, on 12 February 1940, Dad noted 'Left Allery - arrived Berguette", while Alistair wrote 'Left for Berguette on 12 February'.

4. Diary pages 1940.

During those early days in France, Alistair's account also often referred to 'his pals' and 'the three of us' although names were rarely mentioned. Fortunately, the discovery of additional notes referring to Alistair's experiences in France mentioned Dad and Archie by name and we were able to accurately work out the exact occasions when all three of them had been together.

As well as descriptions of events that we now knew were particular to Alistair, Dad and Archie, we gained an insight into what day to day life was like for others in the BEF as they journeyed through northern France. It was a unique record of experiences shared by many in the 153 FA, and we could not have wished to have found a more meaningful and relevant account of those early days. In the months ahead, Alistair's memoirs became an irreplaceable resource as we unravelled our Dad's story.

It was fascinating to uncover details about their experiences but having met Alistair many times over the years and knowing how much our Dad deeply valued his friendship, finding Alistair's wartime recollections was for us also a very personal and poignant reminder of their shared past and lasting friendship.

A month had now passed since we first emailed Alistair's son Stuart in Canada and we had not yet had an answer. As there was no alternative way of making contact with Stuart through the publisher, all we could do now was wait and hope for a reply.

Six

Cornered

Late May to Mid July 1940

As the month of May wore on the German army continued to advance rapidly following their surprise attack through the low countries. The 51st Division were forced to move further and further towards the north coast of France, trying to hold a line almost four times longer than would normally be expected of a division. The 153 FA travelled by road convoy whilst some of the troops journeyed by train.

On 31 May 1940 the *Inverness Courier* included an article entitled: 'Brilliant Rearguard Action.' It goes on to quote from the Ministry of Information announcement of the previous evening:

> 'In view of the increased German pressure on their northern and southern flanks, the statement declared, the BEF had been forced to fall back towards the coast where a battle is now raging. This operation has been carried out with great skill and daring.'[1]

It also went on to say:

> 'British troops are fighting desperately as they withdraw

to the coast through the plain of Flanders. All along the River Yser blazing towns and ruined villages reveal the fury of the engagements between the Allied Armies and the Germans.'[2]

The rearguard action of the British and French troops was described as 'the greatest the world has ever seen.'[3]

Towards the end of May, plans were made to evacuate the entire BEF. From 26 May until 4 June, Operation Dynamo succeeded in evacuating 338,000 Allied troops from Dunkirk. However, 160,000 British troops remained in France, including the 51st Highland Division. By early June the route to Dunkirk was closed for them. On the same day as the last men were evacuated from Dunkirk, the remainder of the BEF, the 51st Division (as part of the French IX Corps) including the French 31st Division engaged with the enemy in the area near Abbeville. Their aim was to try and recapture this important bridgehead on the River Somme, but they were outnumbered and forced to fall back, suffering very heavy casualties.

As a part of the Field Ambulance, we believe Dad travelled through the towns of Beaumont, Campneuseville and Londonières situated to the north of Paris but still well behind the front lines. Even here, however, there was a great deal of enemy aerial activity and movement on the roads was made difficult due to damage from bombs and the large numbers of fleeing refugees.

By 8 June the enemy had managed to cut off the Allies supply base at Rouen. As the Division was no longer in a position to keep fighting, an evacuation plan was formed. The following day the Commander of 154th Brigade (which included 154 Field Ambulance) formed Ark Force and retreated towards Le Havre hoping to hold a line to secure the port for an evacuation attempt.

However, when the German army managed to reach the coast near Fécamp, any hope of evacuating the remainder of the Division from Le Havre had to be abandoned although Ark Force did manage to evacuate over 4000 of its men from here. The situation for the rest of the 51st was now desperate. The only remaining hope was the small fishing port of St Valery-en-Caux although it was far from ideal for an evacuation operation with its small harbour and steep chalk cliffs on both sides of its entrance. The Allies had little choice, however, so they positioned themselves around the outskirts of the town hoping to hold back the enemy long enough to attempt an evacuation by sea.

By 9.00 a.m. the following morning, 11 June, Major General Fortune had sent a message to the Admiralty:

> 'Intend to embark whole force tonight Tuesday provided sufficient ships and boat transport are available. If embarkation cannot be completed tonight propose continuing a.m. tomorrow Wednesday. Estimated numbers 5000 but may reach 10,000. Embarkation tonight considered essential due to probability of attack and shortage of rations, petrol and ammunition.' [4]

By now The Royal Navy had already moved their ships further along the coast towards St Valery-en-Caux and plans were made to try to evacuate the men during the night.

At 10.00 a.m. on the 11th June General Fortune gave this directive to the men:

> 'The Navy will probably make an effort to take us off by boat, perhaps tonight, perhaps in two nights. I wish all ranks to realise that this can only be achieved by the full co-operation of everyone. Men may have to walk five or six miles. The utmost discipline must prevail.' [5]

Everything was sounding quite hopeful for the evacuation but at midday on the 11th, the situation began to change. Despite the Allies best efforts, the German Army had managed to enter St Valery-en-Caux and having swiftly mounted guns on the cliff-tops, were now shelling the town and the harbour area and raking the beaches with machine-gun fire. The naval ships lying off the coast were targeted by airstrikes and enemy fire from cliff-top guns which forced them to move further out from the shore. They still hoped, however, to return closer to the harbour under cover of darkness.

In preparation for their evacuation, the men were ordered to disable any remaining vehicles, weapons and any other equipment no longer required. Late that night, troops were moved to the rendezvous point at the rail station in St Valery-en-Caux with embarkation planned to begin at 2.00 a.m. on the morning of 12 June. It started to rain and as the men gathered, disappointing news awaited them – the evacuation would not take place that night after all – fog had come down delaying the return of the ships. Several boats had in fact already been lost in the battle and the enemy's dominant position on the clifftops made it almost impossible for those remaining to get close enough to the harbour. By now, the whole town was ablaze from enemy shelling and the roads leading in and out of the area were choked with fleeing refugees, burning and broken-down vehicles and rubble from bombed buildings. For the already exhausted men, this news was a severe blow and perhaps many were already guessing that their last chance of escape had now been lost.

On 11 June Dad was still on the eastern outskirts of St Valery-en-Caux where the 153 FA were engaged in collecting the many casualties from the surrounding area. Farm buildings were used as makeshift dressing stations as they did their best to administer first aid in appalling conditions. Alistair describes how at this time they were also under continuous enemy shellfire.

In the early hours of 12 June desperate attempts were made to transfer the wounded men to St Valery-en-Caux in the hope of evacuation. Alistair explains the lead up to his involvement in one of these hastily organised convoys:

> 'An officer then explained that a convoy of ambulances with the wounded was to attempt to reach the coast to be taken off by destroyer. This was the 12th June 1940. The officer stated that he wanted, if possible, volunteers from his own Company and did not want married men. No-one moved and after what seemed an age I was frustrated and impetuous enough to volunteer, even though not in the officer's Company. My offer was accepted and within minutes my pals and several others stepped forward. We

loaded the wounded and drove off in the direction of St Valery.'[6]

During the journey to St Valery-en-Caux an incident took place which both Alistair and our Dad recalled. This was the story that Dad had related to us in the early 1970s of when the ambulance convoy he was with was fired upon by the enemy. As bullets rained down, they were forced to flee from the ambulances with the walking wounded and take cover in the ditches at the side of the road. Dad described some of the terrible injuries the casualties suffered and how there was little they could do to help them as they lay in the ditches waiting for the worst to be over. This particular experience clearly left a very deep impression on him.

Alistair tells the very same story of the ambush in his memoirs, so we know Dad and Alistair shared this horrific experience. Alistair's very full written description not only confirms our Dad's verbal version but gives valuable and fascinating extra detail.

'At the crossroads the convoy stopped and peering through the window into the cab, I noticed the driver was gone. Mortars and bullets crashed and ricocheted wildly. The rear doors were opened and we were ordered into the ditch. The walking wounded were helped into the ditch but efforts to get the stretcher cases out were made impossible under the hail of fire. We had been well and truly ambushed. Crawling back up the ditch we were met by the remainder of the Unit making their way down the road.'[7]

Alistair made separate notes about this event elsewhere in his memoirs:

'Made dash for St Valery with ambulances in early morning. Caught in machine gun fire and trench mortars at crossroads. Lay in ditch for an hour. Unit arrived walking. No officers. Led by BW [Black Watch] officer (wounded) to cliff edge.'

49

5. Illustration showing ambush of ambulance convoy near St Valery-en-Caux.
Sketch by Alistair MacRitchie.
Reproduced by kind permission of George and Stuart MacRitchie

'One of our officers complained that ambulances should not have been fired upon. The answer given was that the Red Crosses were far too small, and the vehicles had to be regarded as troop carriers.'[8]

Alistair was also clearly deeply affected by this ambush and later drew a sketch showing the men cowering in the ditches with the abandoned ambulances on the road. We now knew that the drawing on the cover of *Christmas in the Lager – worse than a Sunday* was indeed Alistair's interpretation of the convoy incident which Dad had been a part of. Later we discovered that Archie too had been there.

Having now reached the cliffs at St Valery-en-Caux, those from the ill-fated ambulance convoy would have been exhausted, shocked by the recent ambush and frightened at how events were turning out for the Division as a whole – but things were about to get even worse.

At 8.00 a.m. on the morning of the 12th, the French Army surrendered. The situation of the 51st Highland Division was now clearly hopeless and Major General Fortune was left with little choice but to agree to surrender also.

6. St Valery-en-Caux in flames, June 1940.
Reproduced by kind permission of Raphaël Distante

All the men were in despair at this turn of events and in disbelief to find themselves unable to escape and awaiting a very uncertain fate. Many also wondered if the war had now been lost. As the German tanks rolled into view, around them the town of St Valery-en-Caux lay in ruins and in flames. Looking out to sea from the clifftops above the town no doubt they could imagine Britain just over the horizon – so tantalisingly close.

The realisation that capture was now inevitable made some men make desperate last-minute attempts to escape by creating makeshift 'ropes' of gun slings to lower themselves down the 300-foot-high cliffs onto the beach below, hoping to then make a dash for the few ships further out at sea. Sadly, many lost their lives as the ropes gave way or were not long enough to reach the ground. In some cases, the enemy cut the ropes so that those on the end fell to their deaths. Others were killed by enemy gunfire and some were forced by the German soldiers to climb back up.

At 11.00 a.m. on the cliff head at St Valery-en-Caux, our father was taken as a prisoner of war, one of almost 10,000 troops captured that day.

A simple one-word entry was all that was written in Dad's diary for Wednesday 12 June 1940:

'Captured'

Casualty figures from around the time of the surrender at St Valery-en-Caux are difficult to confirm but according to various sources it is estimated that around 1000 men died and at least 4000 were wounded.[9]

Although the events at St Valery-en-Caux were reported in the newspapers, the story was not given a high profile at the time. On 14 June 1940 the *Inverness Courier* printed an editorial column which began:

> 'Disappointing though the news is that part of a British Division has been surrounded and cut off on the north coast of Normandy and that six thousand of its men are believed to have been captured by the enemy, and anxious though many at home must be until further details are made known, we must not let either disappointment or anxiety blind us to the fact that in a battle on the immense scale of that now raging in France fluctuations of fortune are bound to occur and must be viewed in their proper perspective whether they are favourable or unfavourable.'[10]

A couple of months later, in August, the *Inverness Courier* also printed the official war office statement describing the gallantry of the 51st (Highland) Division in the great Battle of France which also gave a detailed account of the Divisions movements from the end of May until their capture on 12 June.

All those taken captive were rounded up and marched out of the town to spend their first night in captivity in open fields. Some short distance eastwards along the coast at Veules-les-Roses, a number of men were able to reach the boats lying off the beaches and make their escape.

Other accounts of this fateful day describe how only the very seriously injured men were left behind at St Valery-en-Caux to await transfer to hospital. All the walking wounded were made to join the other POWs on their long march into captivity.

On 13 September 1940, in an article entitled 'Highland Soldiers in Enemy Hands', the *Inverness Courier* reported that:

> 'Private Allan Cameron, R.A.M.C., previously reported missing, is now known to be a prisoner of war in Germany. Before the war he was employed by Messrs Geo. Ross and Noble, solicitors, High Street, Inverness. He is the only son of Mrs A Cameron, 21 Dochfour Drive, Inverness.'

The cutting kept by our grandmother also states that the family of Alistair MacRitchie had received news.

> 'Mr and Mrs G MacRitchie, Fort William, have received word from their younger son Alistair, who was a private in the R.A.M.C.'[11]

The relief for Amelia of knowing Dad, her only son, was still alive must, however, have been tempered by the terrible news that he was now a captive in enemy hands.

The war in Europe continued as the Germans entered Paris, Hitler met with Mussolini and the Soviets began their occupation of the Baltic states.

Both routes are roughly estimated and based mainly on the place names and postcards Dad mentioned in his diary entries, and Alistair's list of towns. Some place names listed below are indicated by numbers on map. (7. Route Map - see page 55)

Le Havre to Saar region - from end of January to early May 1940
Le Havre
Yvetot
Caudebec-en-Caux
Allery
Berguette
Bethune
Haillicourt **(1)**
Don Sainghin **(2)**
Erquinghem-Lys
Armentières **(3)**
Lille **(4)**
La Bassée
Lens
Douai
St Quentin
La Fère
Fressancourt
Laon
Reims
Suippes
Dommartin la Planchette (now Dommartin-Dampierre) **(5)**
Férange
Ising
Aboncourt
Moyeuvre-Grande
Charleville-sous-Bois

Saar region to St Valery-en-Caux - mid May to 12 June 1940
Charleville-sous-Bois
Gisors
Londonières
Campneusseville **(6)**
St Valery-en-Caux

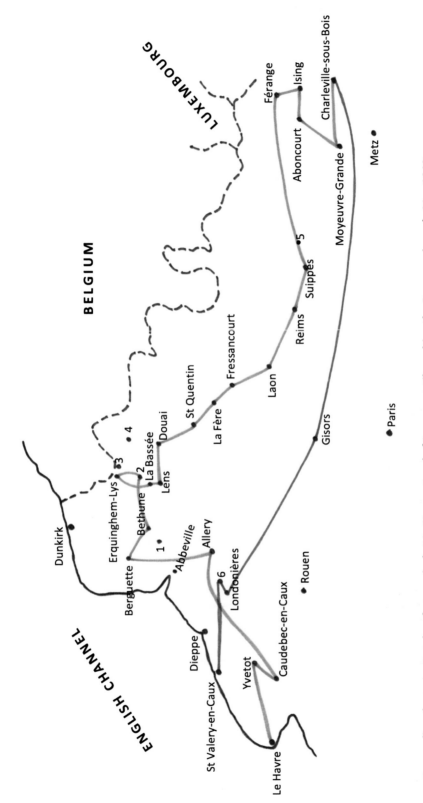

LUXEMBOURG

BELGIUM

ENGLISH CHANNEL

Férange
Ising
Charleville-sous-Bois
Aboncourt
Moyeuvre-Grande
Metz
5
Suippes
Reims
Fressancourt
St Quentin
Laon
La Fère
Douai
4
La Bassée
Lens
3
2
Erquinghem-Lys
Bethune
Gisors
Paris
Dunkirk
1
Abbeville
Allery
Berguette
6
Londonières
Caudebec-en-Caux
Rouen
Dieppe
Yvetot
St Valery-en-Caux
Le Havre

Orange line shows route taken from arrival at Le Havre at end of January until reaching the Saar area in early May 1940.
Green line shows route taken by road party from the Saar area to St Valery-en-Caux from mid-May until 12 June 1940.

A Journey East

In the hours following the surrender, the newly captured soldiers had little time to adjust and many of them were still reeling from the realisation that they were now undeniably Prisoners of War with an uncertain future ahead of them. Already exhausted, hungry and thirsty from the preceding days of intense fighting they were at a low ebb. Hope had now evaporated as they faced the fear of being prisoners, unarmed and surrounded by their captors. It was a desperate situation. Throughout the day, thousands of men were rounded up into makeshift barbed wire enclosures and the following morning were immediately made to start marching, forming a long line as they trudged through northern France. Their journey was to last almost three long and gruelling weeks.

Although Dad had noted some of the place names along the way, Alistair MacRitchie had written a more comprehensive list of towns they passed through in France, Belgium and Holland. As we now knew that Dad was with Alistair both during their capture and the march into captivity, it helped us to form an idea of their route.

France: Buchy, Forges les Eaux, Aumale, Airaines, Doullens, Saint-Paul-sur-Ternoise, Béthune, Seclin, Douai

Belgium: Tournai, Ronse, Aalst, Lokeren

Holland: Dordrecht

The men were formed into lines, up to two miles long and several men abreast. Guards walked or cycled alongside to prevent prisoners from trying to leave the line and to make sure everyone kept up. Distances travelled varied from day to day but usually exceeded the twenty kilometres[12] recommended by The Geneva Convention.[13]

Initially, the men were forced to walk for many hours with very little food and water provided. At the end of a long, hot day they had to sleep mostly in the open fields wearing only the clothes they stood up in. As most of their possessions had either been lost along the way or taken from them during searches, some men became desperate and even resorted to stealing what became prized items of clothing or kit from their fellow POWs. This usually happened at night, so everyone had to take care and keep a close hold of their precious coats and haversacks as they slept!

During the hot days of late June, the POWs became desperately thirsty as they made their way along the dusty roads. As they passed through some of the small towns and villages in the countryside, kindly French women often took pity on the prisoners, leaving out buckets of water for them at the roadsides. However, as the men rushed forwards some German guards took pleasure in cruelly kicking the buckets over and spilling the water. In later years our father recalled how brave and kind the French women were in their efforts to help as they risked being beaten by the guards for trying to assist in this way.

Many accounts tell of how, as the days passed, not only thirst but hunger grew more acute. Becoming increasingly desperate, some tried to grab raw potatoes and sugar beet from fields as they passed or ate bits of mouldy bread they found left on the ground. The raw potatoes in particular caused diarrhoea making some men very ill but such was the longing for food almost anything would be eaten.

Leaving the ranks in an attempt to escape across the fields or even just to try and snatch something edible from the roadside carried the risk of being beaten by the guards or even shot. Despite this, many men became desperate enough to try anyway. Alistair recalled an occasion when he and two friends, who may have been our Dad and Archie, ran into a courtyard and were able to grab some food and drink from the house as well as sheets and blankets. Luckily, they escaped being punished for leaving the line and managed to fill their stomachs. Unfortunately, a guard spotted their blankets and took them away.

> 'With a sneer on his face he walked off, leaving us with a feeling of utter despondency.'[14]

Inability to keep up with the line because of illness, injury or fatigue also brought the increased chance of being beaten or worse. With many becoming exhausted from the long hot marches and the lack of food and water, incidences of cruelty were recounted. The United Nations War Crimes Commission received a number of written testimonies from former POWs who told how they witnessed beatings and even shootings by German guards.[15] Although not every man saw these occurrences take place, almost all the men were aware of what was happening. Most therefore didn't think to attempt to escape but concentrated instead on survival and on putting one foot in front of the other. As the long days passed, they all became more and more worn down and defeated, both physically and mentally.

Several accounts note that the German guards favoured the French prisoners over the British, particularly in relation to food.

'During the first three days the French prisoners were twice fed on tins of sausage and black bread, but no attempt was made to feed the British.'[16]

French prisoners would also often get the first option when any food was made available so that when the British were eventually called forward there would be little or nothing left for them. This was yet another cruel way for the German guards to humiliate and frustrate their British captives.

Alistair MacRitchie notes one similar incident not long after their capture:

'In the afternoon of the second day lorries drew up outside the gates and the Germans aboard them opened the canvas flaps and revealed – bread! There was a mad scramble to the gate where some attempt was made to get into a queue. We expected that at least some system would be used in the distribution, but oh no! It was much more amusing to throw loaves over the gate and watch the proud British fighting like beasts for it! And what wonderful propaganda it would make for Dr Goebbels! The cameras clicked as the mob yelled, screamed and fought!'[17]

At last, after about eighteen days, the men were given a reprieve from the long days of marching. On reaching the Belgian town of Lokeren, many prisoners were loaded into small open wagons, thirty to each, to be transported into Holland on a narrow railway.

Dads first diary entry after June 12 mentions this stage of the journey:

Monday 1st July 1940
Train to Holland - then on board barge

Once in Holland they were transferred onto barges which sailed up the Rhine into Germany as far as the town of Wesel. On papers we received from the International Committee of the Red Cross, it states that Dad was present in a hospital in Lokeren whilst a prisoner of war in German hands. There was no information on why he attended but it must have been only a minor complaint as he continued the journey along with the other prisoners.

Tuesday 2nd July 1940
Still on barge

[According to notes elsewhere in his diary Dad passed through Dordrecht on 2 July]

The men remained on the barges for four days and it was not a pleasant journey as some vessels were filthy with coal dust, and all were overcrowded and lacking any facilities for hygiene. Although Dad gave no details about the barge journey, other accounts (including Alistair MacRitchie's) describe the terrible conditions on board. The continued lack of food and water and the crude sanitary arrangements made the situation even worse.

Thursday 4th July 1940
Still on barge – landed in Germany (noted in separate list as Wesel-on-Rhine)– night march to camp.

From Wesel the men were made to march through the night and eventually reached the city of Dortmund on 5 July where they were taken to the Westfalenhalle, a circular covered sporting arena. Although the original arena was bombed and destroyed in May 1944, it was rebuilt in a similar style after the war.

Dad told us that it was here that men, possibly the French, were reduced to fighting amongst themselves over scraps of food. Many years later, in the early 1990s, our father returned to Dortmund whilst on a visit to Germany and was fortunate to be given access to the building by one of the caretakers, who turned out to have been in the German Army himself in 1940. Both men held a brief conversation in German before shaking hands and although our father did not speak much about this visit at the time, it must nevertheless have brought back vivid memories for him.

Dad also told us stories of German women and children lining the streets shouting insults, jeering and even spitting on the prisoners as they were marched past. Many other POW accounts speak of similar experiences.

The prisoners were kept at Dortmund for four nights.

Friday 5th July 1940
Same camp (Dortmund as in notes)

Tuesday 9th July 1940
Left camp for train

On 9 July our father and most of the other prisoners left Dortmund and were put on board a train. Although they had been looking forward to the prospect of a train journey to save their weary legs, they were soon to be severely disappointed. The 'train' was in fact a series of cattle wagons with the men packed in tightly, fifty to eighty to each wagon, leaving barely any room to sit down.

Dad himself did not describe the conditions on board but many other accounts do. The heat inside the overcrowded wagons was almost unbearable with the doors bolted shut and only a narrow slit near the top to let in any air. They were provided with very little food or water, if any. Many men who had eaten raw potatoes and drunk dirty water were still suffering from upset stomachs and dysentery. There were no toilet facilities and only brief stops for men to relieve themselves. With the journey lasting about thirty-six hours, it was by all accounts a grim experience. Such were the conditions on board that some men died, and their bodies remained inside the wagons until the final destination was reached.

Wednesday 10th July 1940
Train - arrived at permanent camp.

As the German guards shouted 'Raus, Raus!', the men poured out of the wagons onto the platform at Thorn (now known as Toruń) in Poland, physically weak, filthy and extremely hungry and thirsty. In spirit they were defeated and humiliated. Under the guards' commands, they were formed into lines once more and marched to Stalag XXA – they had finally arrived at the prison camp. Stalag was the shortened version of the German word Stammlager (Kriegsgefangenen-Mannschafts-Stammlager was the full name for a prisoner of war camp). POWs sometimes referred to themselves as 'Kriegies'.

A series of seventeen 'forts' surrounding the city of Thorn (Toruń) which dated back to the end of the nineteenth century were built to defend the western border of the kingdom of Prussia. Many of these semi-underground forts were cold, dark and damp. Most also had moats around them.

The town of Thorn had been taken over by the German army in September 1939. Fort VII on the right side of the Vistula river was used as a prison for Polish civilians from the town and surrounding areas whom the Nazis considered a threat.[18] Many of those imprisoned were harshly treated and most were eventually either executed or sent to concentration camps. From the end of October 1939 until December groups of prisoners were taken to the nearby woods at Barbarka on the outskirts of Thorn and executed next to previously dug graves. It is thought that around 1000 people, (Poles and Jews) may have been killed there although in an attempt to hide their war crime the Germans later dug up the bodies and burned them. A memorial now stands at the site commemorating the victims.

Just a few months later, during the first half of 1940, the Germans had begun using a number of other forts, all on the left side of the

Vistula, to hold the growing number of Allied POWs. However, in July they had not expected to have captured such a great number of prisoners and were forced to hastily erect overflow accommodation. Wooden huts were built close to the forts, each containing bunk beds for up to fourteen men. It was the huts next to Fort 11, known as Camp 11A, where Dad was first sent, and he remained there for almost three weeks during which time he was 'processed'. All new prisoners had to be officially registered on arrival at the POW camps.

Friday 12th July 1940
Wrote PC's home. Reported specs. Alistair and Archie went to hospital.

We know from Alistair's account that he and Archie were admitted to the hospital shortly after arrival to be treated for scabies and remained there for several days.

Tuesday 16th July 1940
Photos, numbers, registration etc

8 days later:

Head shaved!

As part of the registration process the POWs were fingerprinted and also had their photographs taken holding a board with their new prisoner of war number written on it. Metal identity discs were issued and were meant to be worn at all times. All men were deloused and also had their heads shaved.

Under the terms of the *Geneva Convention 1929*, Article 36, prisoners were to be given the opportunity to send a postcard home within a week of their arrival in a POW camp.

'Not later than one week after his arrival in camp, and similarly in case of sickness, each prisoner shall be enabled to send a postcard to his family informing them of his capture and the state of his health.'[19]

We have a copy of the 'capture card' Dad completed which would have been sent to his next of kin. He would also have filled in a

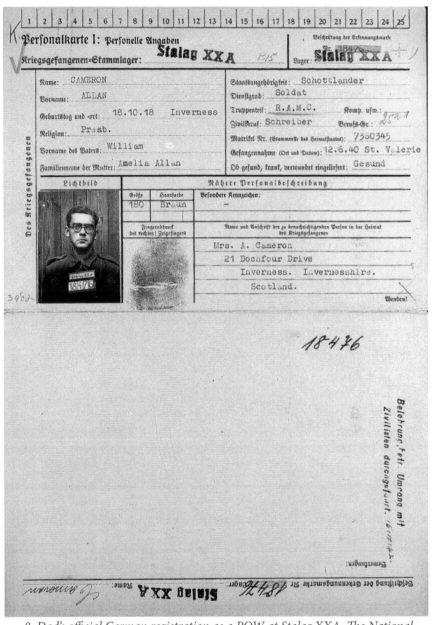

8. *Dad's official German registration as a POW at Stalag XXA. The National Archives, ref. WO 416/55/148. Reproduced by kind permission of Imperial War Museum.*

separate card to be sent to the International Committee of the Red Cross (ICRC) who kept records of all men who had been captured. The ICRC had their headquarters in Geneva and their main responsibility was to protect and assist POWs and ensure that their treatment met the standards of the *Geneva Convention*.[20]

Now that Dad was officially registered as a POW he had to learn to adjust to and accept the realities of his imprisonment. No doubt he would have felt both apprehension and uneasiness about what might lie ahead.

Seven

Alan Moore

Late December 2011 to March 2012

Arrival at Stalag XXA marked an abrupt end to five months of zigzagging and backtracking across northern Europe. Dad, Alistair and Archie had managed to stay together but it had been a grim experience as they witnessed the devastation and loss of life that took place when British and French troops were forced to take rearguard action against the German forces leading up to their capture at St Valery-en-Caux.

In Alistair's memoirs we had discovered the circumstances surrounding the ambush on the ambulance convoy that had left such an impression on Dad. We could only admire and feel proud of all those who had been prepared to volunteer and risk their own lives by accompanying the wounded to the coast for evacuation. It reminded us of the countless acts of bravery we had read about and the tragic loss of life that had occurred at St Valery-en-Caux and knowing that these events had sealed the fate of many thousands of men we wondered why we, and many of our contemporaries, knew so little about what had happened just a few miles along the coast from Dunkirk. Outside of military institutions and a handful of books it seemed that there was little known by our generation about the Battle

65

of France and the involvement of the 51st Highland Division. Even some historians have only mentioned in passing the fact that thousands of men were still fighting in France ten days after the Dunkirk evacuation.

It was now mid-December, Christmas preparations were under way, and we were making progress with our Dad's account as he described the process of beginning life as a POW. Yet, we were curious, as, shortly after his arrival in Thorn, we noticed there appeared to be now another POW mentioned in the diary. It seemed that Dad had possibly met another inmate whose initial was 'A' as on 29 July he had written, '...A. A. A. and self moved out to fort 15.'

Assuming that Alistair and Archie were two of the POWs being moved out to 'Fort 15' with Dad, the third 'A' was a mystery. Further entries note: 'Alan M admitted to hospital...' 'AM still sick' and 'A Moore went to work in wood-yard'. Our guess was that these entries possibly referred to an inmate called 'Alan Moore.'

It was confusing as Alistair's initials were AM and Alistair and Archie were both also usually referred to as 'A' in Dad's notes. After a quick check through Alistair's diary extracts it showed that he too had mentioned someone else, apart from our father, called 'Allan.' Although the spelling was different, both accounts contained the same information about an 'Alan' or 'Allan' on exactly the same date.

We were now intrigued to find out more about this fourth person and a general internet search using the few facts that were available to us showed an article that had been published in the *Daily Telegraph*. It featured a recent episode of the popular Antiques Roadshow television series in which members of the public are invited to have their antiques and collectables valued. On Sunday 13 November 2011 the BBC had broadcast an Antiques Roadshow Remembrance Special that had been filmed at the National Arboretum in Staffordshire. This particular programme focused on wartime stories.

The newspaper article was primarily concerned with highlighting Prince Andrew's involvement in the Falklands War but halfway through it said,

'The programme also features a story of Alan Moore, 92, a veteran of the Second World War, who reveals the extraordinary story behind a 70-year-old secret that kept him and others alive with hope.'[1]

The feature explained that Alan Moore, from Truro in Cornwall, had been in the RAMC and was attached to the Field Ambulance (FA) with the 51st Highland Division which was sent to France as part of the BEF. He was eventually captured at St Valery-en-Caux, endured a three-week journey to Thorn in Poland and then spent five years as a POW in Stalag XXA.

The similarities in Alan Moore's reported story to what we knew of Dad's and Alistair's experiences were clear. Yet we were aware that thousands of men had been captured at St Valery-en-Caux and that a staggering number of around 60,000 POWs had passed through Stalag XXA during the war years. However, Alan's connection to the RAMC and the FA seemed an extraordinary coincidence.

Understandably we were now keen to hear the complete Antiques Roadshow interview and after eventually locating the Remembrance Special programme online we were at last able to hear Alan Moore's fascinating WW2 story for ourselves.

While incarcerated in Stalag XXA in Poland, Alan had risked his life after successfully managing to smuggle a radio into the camp. With the help of the Polish resistance the radio was brought in with the undertaker and in return one hundred cigarettes were placed under a corpse as payment. Once inside the camp, the radio was kept hidden behind a loose brick in an inside wall. Secretly tuning into the BBC news helped to keep up the morale of fellow prisoners as they listened to updates of the Allies progress. Astonishingly, Alan had managed to bring the radio safely back to the UK after the war and on a visit to Poland a few years ago had found the exact loose brick and cavity that had kept his radio hidden.

It was a remarkable story and although no name was given during the interview the facts matched The Telegraph's article. We had both been aware of the original television broadcast in November but as we were still in the early stages of gathering information, Stalag XXA had little significance to us at that time.

As we listened to the interview, we were surprised to discover that Alan Moore had also been in the 153 FA – the same Field Ambulance unit as our Dad. Having recently found Alistair's memoirs, the possibility that we may have discovered a former POW who may have known Dad, Alistair and Archie seemed too much to hope for after all this time and family and friends also had reservations about our optimism! We too had our doubts as there was no evidence of anyone in our father's wartime snaps resembling the photo of 'Alan as a POW' which was shown on the BBC programme. Yet, even if it turned out not to be the person Dad had known, we felt it would still be a unique and exciting opportunity to make contact with a fellow captive from Stalag XXA.

Over Christmas we finally decided to contact the Antiques Roadshow to explain that we had recently watched their interview with a WW2 veteran and were curious to find out if it was indeed the person mentioned in our late father's diaries. One week later we received a response.

> '...I shall forward your email on to Alan where I'm sure it will be met with interest and gratitude. I hope some interesting correspondence ensues for you...'[2]

(Junior Researcher, Antiques Roadshow, 13 January 2012)

This was encouraging news! Now we just had to wait and hope for a reply.

In the meantime, we busied ourselves transcribing the final section of Dad's 1940 diary, reading Alistair's detailed memoirs of those first few months in German-occupied Poland and researching other veteran's accounts of Stalag XXA. For the prisoners in Poland it was the start of an unforgiving winter of hardship. For us, winter was gradually giving way to spring, thoughts of warmer weather and trips away from home.

While on a short February break there was an alert from home to say that an unexpected message had been left on the answering machine. It seemed that Alan Moore had been in touch and wanted to speak to us.

It had been six weeks since we had first contacted the Antiques Roadshow and we were cautiously optimistic that this could be the reply we had been hoping for. Now we only had to wait two more days before we were able to listen to the phone message for ourselves.

> 'This is Alan Moore here. I'm the Alan Moore you're looking for and of course I remember your father... Allan Cameron....'

Nothing could have prepared us emotionally for hearing Alan's message for the first time. Even now the memory of what he said remains as clear and vivid as ever. To discover that not only had Alan known Dad but could also remember him after so many years took us completely by surprise.

We were elated to have found Alan but there was a feeling of sadness too as our thoughts turned to our Dad who was not here to share this moment. He, we felt sure, would have been thrilled to know that his long-forgotten diaries had led us to find his POW friend. Now that Alan had made contact, we were delighted to learn that he was keen to hear from us.

Two days had already passed since the message had been left on the answering machine and we were anxious to return the call as soon as possible. However, we were not quite sure what to expect as, aside from what had been broadcast on the programme, we only had some sketchy diary notes which gave glimpses of the day-to-day life that Alan had once shared with Dad, Alistair and Archie to go on.

We need not have worried. When we spoke to Alan and his wife Hilda that evening the conversation flowed seamlessly. They were a delight to talk to and there was a fascinating story to hear as Alan spoke about his past.

During that first phone call we heard some of Alan's own extraordinary personal story as he talked about what he had experienced and seen first-hand. He recalled vivid memories of tragic scenes when lives were lost at St Valery-en-Caux and it seemed that there was more hardship in the camps than we had first gleaned from our father's carefully self-censored diaries.

Alan explained that he had met Dad, Alistair and Archie when they had first arrived at Stalag XXA and knew them all well as they had spent many months together. We also heard recollections about the dangerous circumstances that Alan found himself in at the end of the war. As we listened to his account, we began to understand more about the reality of what it had been like for many of those who had been taken prisoner and marched into years of captivity.

Yet Alan was also keen to know what had become of his friends after the war and we were glad that we were at least able to shed some light on Dad's and Alistair's post-war history. There was a chance to explain how our father's diaries had led us to Alan and he was surprised and pleased to hear that we also had discovered Alistair's memoirs and were currently trying to find a way to contact his sons, Stuart and George MacRitchie.

As for Archie Dey ... there was little we could say. Apart from a hazy recollection of a conversation with our aunt Jean, who thought that Archie may have at one time had connections in Ayrshire or Canada, we had no knowledge of his post-war whereabouts.

Before our phone call came to an end Alan and Hilda had an unexpected proposition for us. If all was well, they suggested that we should try and meet up in the summer... 'somewhere in Scotland!' Both Hilda and Alan were in good health and active, so travelling was not an issue. Remarkably, at the age of ninety-two, Alan still worked part-time and frequently drove to the south of England. We were also pleased to discover that Alan and Hilda lived, not in Truro, Cornwall, but in North Yorkshire. This was good news as it reduced travelling distances for everyone, making it easier to organise a meeting.

In the meantime, we arranged to forward a copy of Alistair's memoirs, a transcript of Dad's diaries when they were complete, and a promise to keep them up to date about any further developments. As we came to terms with what had seemed an extraordinary and impossible turn of events, we could not have wished for a better outcome.

Eight

Waiting

Late July 1940 to March 1941

Following Dad's POW registration process at Stalag XXA there was a short period of time where the new prisoners were kept entertained by talks and presentations;

Thursday 25th July 1940
Toc H lecture

Friday 26th July 1940
Interesting lecture on the fishing industry – Grimsby etc,
Names of RAMC personnel taken by Germans.

As we tried to discover why the names of RAMC personnel were noted by the Germans we found out that, under the terms of the *Convention for the Amelioration of the Condition of the Wounded and Sick in Armies in the Field (Geneva Convention 1929)*, medical personnel were to be considered 'protected' although in many cases this 'protection' was not put into practice.

'Art. 9. The personnel charged exclusively with the removal, transportation, and treatment of the sick and

72

wounded, as well as with the administration of sanitary formations and establishments, and the chaplains attached to armies, shall be respected and protected under all circumstances. If they fall into the hands of the enemy, they shall not be considered prisoners of war.'[1]

The Report of the ICRC on its activities during the Second World War, Volume 1 further recommends that 'they shall be repatriated, as soon as a route for their return is open and military considerations permit'[2] although there was also an agreement that a number of the medical personnel should remain in the camps in order to look after their fellow POWs.

Many medical personnel became prisoners during the war as they tended to stay with the wounded men. We know that RAMC was recorded on our father's German registration card and his name would therefore have been included on the list taken on 26 July.

Sunday 28th July 1940
Cards! – service at 7.30pm in tent – first party of farm workers ready to leave on Monday (29th).

On Sunday 14 and 28 July Dad notes that he took part in religious services. He would have drawn comfort from this as he enjoyed attending church regularly and was registered as Presbyterian on his service papers.

He also mentions that work parties were already being formed and groups of men were preparing to leave the main camp. Stalag XXA (see Appendix 1 for details of individual Forts) administered a number of sub-camps or Arbeitskommando [labour camps] which were situated at various work locations, usually in the neighbouring towns or on farms in the surrounding countryside. All records for the outlying detention centres were maintained by the headquarters at Stalag XXA which from around the time that Dad arrived at Thorn was located in a two-storey house opposite Fort XIII (now Okolna Street). Prisoners below the rank of sergeant, including Dad who was a private, were sent to work at these sub-camps and therefore did not spend all their time at the main Stalag. Accommodation was provided at the satellite camps and could vary considerably. Once a particular job or contract was completed the men would normally be returned to Stalag XXA until such time as they were detailed for another work party so there could be up to three thousand men living in the main camp at any time. The Thorn complex was itself a sub-camp of the concentration camp in Stutthof (now Sztutowic)[3] which lay to the north of Thorn near Danzig (now Gdansk).

Monday 29th July 1940
First farm party left – A.A.A. (Alistair, Archie, Alan) and self moved out to Fort 15 (300 of us) - Ukrainians etc (swapping)

The friends were still together when they were moved to Fort XV but as the first work parties were already being detailed for work away from Thorn, they must have been anxious to hear what was to happen with them and if they would now be separated. Many POWs were used as farm labourers and perhaps our father expected that was where he would also be sent.

Dad mentions Ukrainians at Fort XV and Alistair tells of tensions as the Ukrainians already accommodated there were made to give up their boots for the arriving British POWs. Ethnic Ukrainians were among millions of people taken to Germany from Central and Eastern Europe to be used as forced labour. These Ostarbeiter (Eastern workers) often lived in guarded camps, were given meagre rations and made to work long hours for German industries.[4]

Wednesday 31st July 1940
Letter cards home

It seems that Dad might have been quite fortunate to get a letter card to write and send home as the postal and censorship services in Germany had been overwhelmed by the huge numbers of new POWs and had in fact been temporarily suspended during June 1940. In an attempt to limit the amount of mail sent and received, the POWs were restricted to sending two letters and four postcards each month. In addition to heavy censorship by the German authorities, the letter cards and postcards both had limited space for writing.

Dad had been a POW for less than two months when he received notification for his first work detail and preparations were made for leaving Stalag XXA.

Thursday 1st August 1940
Issue of boots prior to leaving.

However, a welcome surprise came first:

Friday 2nd August 1940
Red Cross parcels of food (Weetabix and fruit)

Red Cross parcels were hugely important to the POWs, not only because they provided a vital supplement to their sparse food rations but also because they were an indication from the outside world that they had not been forgotten. By the end of the war twenty million parcels had been sent to POWs. Packing took place at the Prisoners of War Department in the UK and the parcels were then shipped to Lisbon or Marseilles. With the assistance of the International Committee of the Red Cross (ICRC), they were transferred by rail to Geneva and finally distributed to the various prison camps throughout Europe and beyond. In a building next to the Stalag XXA headquarters, mail was collected, and International Red Cross parcels were sorted before being distributed to the various labour camps. The Red Cross also sent out next of kin parcels and packages containing educational books and even sports equipment. There can be no doubt that these items greatly improved the quality of life for many of the POWs.

The *Inverness Courier* printed a paragraph about the Red Cross in its 26 January 1940 edition:

> 'Scottish prisoners of war in enemy hands are to be cared for by the Red Cross [...] Packing depots will be established in various parts of Scotland and at these depots 'approved packers' will prepare the parcels for the prisoners of war. Private parcels, sent by relatives, must be repacked at those depots. The Red Cross is the only organization which can perform this service, since, by the Geneva Convention, it is a neutral body.'[5]

Later in the year they were able to confirm that the Scottish Branch of the British Red Cross Society had received news from the HQ in London that parcels for POWs were reaching Geneva ready for distribution. In October a plea was made for donations:

'The need of contributions to enable the Red Cross to keep up a steady flow is extremely urgent, . . . a much larger amount is required. It is hoped, therefore, that all classes of the community will make it a point of honour to contribute to the fund, especially as so many men from this part of the world are prisoners in Germany.' [6]

Graudenz

Thursday 3rd August 1940
Left fort at 3am - train journey of 2 hours - prospect of work - new fort

Leaving Thorn in the early hours of the morning, once again in cattle trucks, Dad, Archie Dey, Alistair MacRitchie and Alan Moore began the sixty-kilometre journey to the town of Graudenz (now known by its Polish name of Grudziądz) which lay to the north-east of Thorn. Dad was to spend almost twelve months here.

Many sub-camps, like this one, were not traditional POW camps but were civilian buildings taken over and used as accommodation centres. Heavy bombing in 1945 destroyed over sixty per cent of the city so it proved difficult for us to find any further information about the actual place Dad stayed in. Alistair MacRitchie mentions in his memoirs that on arrival in Graudenz they were marched to a building with iron bars at the windows and a barbed wire enclosure all around it. He was led to believe it was formerly an offender's institution although other accounts mention that POWs were sent to a former poorhouse. Inside there were no beds or blankets, just makeshift pallets with straw to lie on.

Although not sharing the same room, all four men still saw each other every day whilst out on work parties and therefore spent a good deal of time together.

Settling in as best as they could in their new surroundings, it is unlikely that the POWs were fully aware of the terrible atrocities that had taken place in and around Graudenz just over one year before, following its capture on 4 September 1939. As in Thorn, members of the Selbstschutz Organization, under direction of the SS, had rounded up Polish civilians and used the building of a former boarding school in Graudenz as a holding camp for these prisoners. Many were then sent to concentration camps whilst others were murdered either by shooting or beating. In Graudenz a public execution in the town park was held as a means of intimidation.[7]

Sunday 4th August 1940
No church service (no blankets)

From reading the diaries we discovered that Sunday was usually a rest day. Dad enjoyed attending church services, so he was disappointed to find that they were far from regular at Graudenz. According to Article 16 of The Geneva Convention, POWs 'shall be permitted complete freedom in the performance of their religious duties, including attendance at the services of their faith.'[8] The ICRC received many complaints from the POWs about the inadequacy of religious support and they requested that service chaplains should be based in each main camp and make regular visits to the neighbouring labour detachments.

The lack of blankets which Dad mentions remained a problem for quite some time as almost three weeks later on Sunday 25 August he writes:

Day off – cold again - still no blankets or towels

On Monday 5 August the first of the work parties were sent out and the following day it was Dad's turn:

Tuesday 6th August 1940
First day's work - cleaning up river bank etc - dirty job.

Saturday 10th August 1940
Working on dump in town - weeding

For the remainder of August, he carried out various labouring jobs including cleaning up the riverbank, working on the dump in town, and weeding on the bank of a stream. During these early days at Graudenz Dad and his three friends were all sick at different times – no doubt the effects of poor living conditions, hard manual labour and a lack of good food.

Monday 12th August 1940
Archie sick

Wednesday 14th August 1940
Archie still sick. Alan M admitted to hospital

Saturday 24th August 1940
Alistair and I both sick - I with glasses – no work – cold, wet, miserable day

On a brighter note, Dad mentions one big bonus of working in the outdoors:

Work on bank of stream - apples, tomatoes etc in orchard

..buckshee loaves while at car park!

… large loaf pinched by fellow worker!!!

Towards the end of August, the American Red Cross issued cheeses, cigarettes, tins of beef and tinned milk. Like the British Red Cross parcels, these supplements to their frugal diet were hugely important, although the parcels usually had to be shared between several people.

Tuesday 27th August 1940
Work – issue of 3 cheeses & 10 Gold Dollar cigs (cheeses delicious) from American Red Cross

Wednesday 28th August 1940
Work - issue of 1 cheeses, 2 fifths of tin of beef, 3 cigarettes, tin milk from American Red Cross (milk best of all)

Thursday 29th August 1940

Work, 1lb marmalade, 4 pkts of Ovo Sport (very good) from American Red Cross

Friday 30th August 1940

No work - deloused - half tin of sausage, bar of chocolate and cocoa from American Red Cross.

A recurring theme in many accounts of POW life and something which our father told us about himself was the problem of lice. All the men were afflicted by them at some point and although they tried their best to get rid of them by burning them out from the seams of their clothes or squashing them between their fingers this only gave temporary relief. Sometimes they even had competitions to see who could kill the most lice at one sitting! Living in close quarters with many other men, the lack of facilities for washing and their basic living conditions all combined to make it virtually impossible to eradicate them altogether. The German guards carried out regular delousing sessions on the men and the accommodation huts in an effort to keep the lice under control and to prevent outbreaks of typhus.

Dad made an entry in his diary for every day of September and the monotony of their day-to-day lives was now becoming apparent. He spent the entire month 'ditching' on the riverbanks but also struck up friendships with Poles who were part of his work party. One young Polish man in particular, who we think may have been called Karl, was very generous towards Dad and was first mentioned in the last entry for August:

showed young Pole my photos etc – discussed my profession.

In the days following, interactions with the Polish prisoners and civilians are mentioned on several occasions;

Work again - generosity of young Pole towards me - tomatoes (for lad with glasses), sandwich from his own lunch, rolls & bread, coffee from farm

Coffee and sandwiches (ham) from Poles

1 packet of tobacco & cig paper from Poles

young Pole still decent

Ditching on river with young Pole - incident of sandwiches - gave me package of sandwiches taken from one of the lads as I had no bread

Young Pole allowed Alistair and I to sit by Polish women on seat

At the end of the month there is one final mention of Karl;

Monday 30th September 1940
Karl left to join Labour Corps

Although the work was often hard, having contact with the Polish people gave the men an opportunity to hear more about what was happening in the outside world as well as the chance to receive gifts of food which they either smuggled back into camp or ate whilst out working:

Saturday 14th September 1940
Ditching – no Pole in charge – knocked off at 10 o'clock owing to rain – cognac, coffee & roll on farm. Bread & rolls in canteen

Near the beginning of September Dad mentions festival preparations which are taking place:

preparation of town for festival – flags etc

and on 3 September,

Nazi festival preparations in town

The following day,

Wednesday 4th September 1940
Holiday - Nazi celebration in town - sweets arrived in canteen

We do not know for sure what this 'festival' was for, but we learned that the City Council of Graudenz surrendered to the German Army on this day in 1939. The area around Graudenz was first attacked by German forces on 1 September and captured completely by 4 September so this 'celebration' was probably to commemorate that military victory.

Thursday 5th September 1940

Work as usual – ditching. Coffee and sandwiches (ham) from Poles –jam & sugar issue at night.

Although the majority of Dad's work this month was ditching yet again, on occasion he was given additional tasks, for example:

Friday 6th September 1940

Heavy work carrying granite.

Around this time, we also start to hear reports of items 'appearing' in Alistair's haversack!

Monday 23rd September 1940

Ditching. Alistair got his haversack with bread and apples

Tuesday 24th September 1940

Ditching - bought loaf with Jerry money that Alistair got in his haversack yesterday.

Thursday 26th September 1940

Piece of bread in Alistair's bag.

We believe the system employed was to leave the empty bag or haversack in a particular place so that the local 'friend' could put something into it for them, usually food of some sort. The bag would later be collected by the POW before heading back to the camp at the end of their work shift. If they were lucky the bag would not be searched by the guards and they could share whatever was in it between them.

We also start to hear talk of 'buckshees' - items of food mainly, which they were able to procure when out on work parties - apples from orchards for example or loaves of bread given to them by locals. The importance to the men of obtaining these extra bits of food became very clear when we saw how often it was noted down.

sardines for tea (i.e., Archies buckshees)

heavy rain & shelter in farm – buckshees

Sunday 22nd September 1940
Lovely service held in dining hall with German medical orderly as Chaplain ('telling service')

This was the first service held at Graudenz which both Dad and Alistair attended and enjoyed very much.

The following Wednesday brought a very welcome delivery of two hundred and fifty Red Cross parcels which were distributed the following day - one between two. For the next three evenings Dad dined well!

Thursday 26th September 1940
…. Red Cross parcels issued – one between two. Beef stew, sausage, milk powders, celery, meat roll, choc, sweets, syrup, sugar, rice, Yorkshire pudding mixture, margarine, herrings, blackcurrant puree, salt, soap

Friday 27th September 1940
Beef stew for tea (very tasty)

Saturday 28th September 1940
Pork sausage for tea (delicious)

Sunday 29th September 1940
Made rice pudding & chicken roll & salad for tea (mayonnaise delicious)

Although Dad had written a number of letter cards home, up until now he had not received any mail in return. He probably did not know if any of his letters had actually reached Inverness. Reassuring letters from family members and friends at home were eagerly awaited by all the captured men and they welcomed any news from the world they had left behind. One of the tasks undertaken by the ICRC was to keep the British Red Cross informed on delays in delivery of prisoner's mail and act as a postal relay station when required.[9]

12th September 1940
Ditching on river with young Pole – issue of letter cards – strange dream of my dear father – in uniform in Lower Kessock Street

Dad was still a very young boy when his father died so although he had few real memories of him, he would have seen the studio photographs of his father in uniform which his mother displayed. As he sat to write his lettercards home, his thoughts may have turned to family and friends and perhaps this prompted him to dream of his father and of his childhood days in Lower Kessock Street.

As the month wore on the Polish winter started to bite:

issue of coats

work on river as usual – very cold. Work coats for first time…

coats again (cold)

During October Dad filled in an entry for every day of the month. The river work continued and there are several references to how much colder the weather had become - indeed winter underwear was now issued in addition to the work coats received a couple of weeks earlier.

got issued with long underpants! Very cold

Although Dad does not say who provided the extra garments, it may have been through the Red Cross as, in addition to food parcels, they also arranged for clothing supplies to be sent to the prisoners.

For a period of time Dad is lucky to receive food from the Poles most mornings whilst out working although he also speaks of boiling potatoes at night in the camp, sometimes even potato peelings. The river work was for the town corporation and they also supplied some rations.

Both Alan Moore and Alistair report sick.

Wednesday 2nd October 1940

Horlicks (delicious) & coffee, sandwiches, rolls etc at 10 o'clock. Canteen reopened for razor blades etc, bought boot polish

Friday 4th October 1940

Working on river. No coffee or bread at 10 o'clock – Alan M sick again (chill)

Saturday 5th October 1940

Working on river. Coffee & cheese sandwiches & apples at 10 o'clock. AM still sick. Alistair sick with rheumatism

Sunday 6th October 1940

No work. No service – inspected by Kommandant.

Monday 7th October 1940

Working on river again – sandwiches & rolls at 10 o'clock. No coffee. Alistair still got rheumatism in his knees – ordered to bed for 2 days.

Friday 11th October 1940

Alistair back at work. Boiled potatoes at night again

Sunday 13th October 1940

No work. No service – boiled some potato peelings in the camp

Monday 14th October 1940

Work on river again – no bread or rolls from the Poles today – had tin of boiled potatoes

Although keeping well generally, Dad mentions having a tooth filled by the dentist and he also lost a lens from his glasses in the river.

Work on river again – coffee and bread at ten – lost one lens of my glasses in the river – got 2 slices of bread from the guard – very cold!!!

New guards came on duty for the outdoor work parties on 10

October and again on 28 October. Sometimes they were lucky, and the guards would show some small kindnesses to the POWs:

Guard bought packet of cigs for us (half a cig each)

I got 2 slices of bread from guard with glasses – same guard bought a loaf for the party.

got 2 slices of bread from the guard

Dad's 22nd birthday was a day just like any other:

Friday 18th October 1940
Work till nine then deloused - back about 12.30. Very cold. MY BIRTHDAY TODAY - 22!

Food still remained one of the main topics in Dad's diary:

Coffee and one fifth of a loaf from the corporation at 10am - bread etc from Poles

Dripping at night

full bowls of soup today

tin of boiled spuds and carrots at night

increased rations of soup

coffee and bread at tea

Dad noted down a typical day's rations:

MENU IN FORT XXA 51	
5.30am	Coffee & bread - 1/3 or 1/4 loaf
12 noon	Soup - carrot, barley, peasemeal, cabbage, cauliflower, macaroni, spinach, turnip, dried veg etc
4.30pm	Issue of dripping or lard or jam; cheese or sausage
5.00pm	Coffee with sugar
7-8pm	Biscuits (if being issued in lieu of bread) -55 to 60 each

Biscuits were sometimes issued in lieu of bread and according to Dad's notes they received these about every two weeks. The 'coffee' was in fact a substitute often made from ground acorns.

POWs were meant to receive the same rations as the German civilian population but in practice the rations were much less than this and in fact were reduced even further when civilian restrictions were imposed. The ICRC received many complaints from POWs about food rations and negotiations to improve the situation were almost continual from 1940 onwards. Relief supplies of International Red Cross food parcels were increased but the German authorities then used this increase as an excuse to gradually reduce their basic POW ration. A request was therefore made that relief supplies should not be counted as part of their daily allowance.[10] The many lists of food parcel contents featured in Dad's diaries demonstrates how all-consuming the issue of rations was, not only for him but for all the men.

Monday 28th October 1940
Work on river – new guards – Red Cross Parcels issued (2 between 13 men) – got sausages & beans & sugar for tea

Tuesday 29th October 1940
Worked until 3pm – Palethorpes sausages for tea – very cold

Wednesday 30th October 1940
Sausages and beans for tea

On the last Sunday of October –

No work - no service - full bowls of soup today - issue of 60 Junak cigs - honey issue - 1/8 of a box - bible class in afternoon - most enjoyable

As Dad and his friends began their fourth month as POWs, they were kept hard at work mostly toiling on the river which included such tasks as loading brushwood, wiring posts and working on the path next to the water. Occasionally he was detailed to do potato pitting in the camp and on one occasion sawing wood in the woodyard, but mostly Dad was labouring outside in the increasingly cold and wet weather. Most of the time he was alongside his three friends but, as they had no say when working parties were allocated by the guard, sometimes they were separated.

Wednesday 6th November 1940
Separated from Archie and Alistair & put on road party - no coffee or bread - Alan M went to sick bay - bad circulation - dripping & cheese

Tuesday 26th November 1940
Got separated from river party today - working in woodyard

Despite the bitterly cold weather, at least when working outside the camp there was the chance of some 'buckshees' and interaction with the Poles.

Tuesday 5th November 1940
Work on river - roasted spuds - raining most of day - each got a buckshee soup (barley)

Thursday 7th November 1940
Alistair & I got buckshee soup each - dripping & sausage. Pole ('Los') asked what I did in civvy life

An unexpected opportunity arose in early November:

Friday 8th November 1940
Work on river – wiring – coffee & bread & a few roasted spuds – got some rags out of old theatre at river (foot cloths etc) – dripping & sausage

Some of these rags from the theatre were useful to wrap around their feet for extra warmth when working outdoors.

All the men were issued with metal identity discs when they were registered as POWs and were required to wear them at all times. At one point when working on the river job, Dad lost his identity disc and although he never refers to this again he must have had it replaced soon after.

87

Saturday 9th November 1940

Work on river – wrote two postcards home – lost my identity disc – dripping & sausage – I got buckshee Jerry soup – Archie & Alistair got peasemeal

A religious service on 3 November was the only one held during that month.

Sunday 3rd November 1940

No work – service held at 9.30am and with German medical orderly acting as chaplain (very good) – concert at night in dining hall (very good) – sausage issue

With the help of the Red Cross's Indoor Recreations, Fiction, Music and Games Section, musical instruments were acquired and those with talent put them to good use. Eventually, bands were formed, and concerts organised by the POWs started to become a regular feature – sometimes even the guards joined in!

Sunday 10th November 1940

No work – early reveille – three of us making blinds – got soup each – concert at night – two Jerries gave a song

Both Dad and Alistair mention the Armistice commemorations on 11 November which we assume were conducted by a military chaplain.

Monday 11th November 1940

Work on river – Archie & I got buckshee soup & a lot of mail arrived – held 2 min silence at 11am – Armistice service at night

During November 1940 Dad was given dripping and cheese or dripping and sausage for his main evening meal every night for ten days;

Thursday 14th November 1940

Work on river – hours changed i.e. 8am to 3pm – rained a lot – issue of 60 Junak fags – sausage & dripping

Friday 15th November 1940

Work on river – still wiring posts – very mild – sausage &

dripping – Archie got buckshee

Saturday 16th November 1940
Work on river – rather foggy – cheese & dripping

The tedium of Dad's daily routine is apparent now and it is easy to understand why the Red Cross food parcels became so important to the men when you read how basic the food rations provided were.

Around the middle of November however, there was one particular highlight for Dad:

Sunday 17th November 1940
No service - three of us mending blinds - received my first letter from MOTHER dated 25th July - got 2 buckshee soups. Red Cross parcels (one between 8 men) got herring, B Vita - issue of beetroot, salt & soap today

Dad was obviously delighted to have received his first letter from his mother and to know all was well at home, even if the news was four months old!

For the next two days, Dad stayed in the camp as he had reported his boots as faulty and they had to be mended.

Tuesday 19th November 1940
Not working - boots still in cobblers - on potato pitting in camp - more Red Cross parcels arrived - sausage & dripping issue - apricots & milk & biscuits for supper - had B Vita [Bournvita]

The following day he was back out working but he refers to the fact that 'two lads tried to escape today (put in coal cellar)'. As far as we know Dad never made any escape attempts himself but there are many stories about others who did try. Punishments for attempting to escape varied considerably – perhaps a spell in the cellar was one of the more lenient ones!

Wednesday 20th November 1940
Back on river again – different part – rumour that more Red Cross had arrived – had stew for tea

Thursday 21st November 1940
*Work on river again – issue of soap & Red Cross parcels
(one parcel to 6 men) – I drew syrup & milk – dripping &
cheese (crowdie) with buckshee soup each*

The guards who watched them whilst they were out with the working parties were changed regularly and some were more well disposed towards the prisoners than others;

*guard gave pkt of tobacco between us' and the following day
'guard gave tobacco again*

Many of the men smoked whilst in the POW camps and Dad was no exception. Amongst the few items he brought home with him after the war was a canvas roll-up pouch containing pockets to hold a cigarette roller, filter tips and presumably tobacco. There were also packets of Rizla cigarette papers still inside. Throughout the diaries there are many references to issues of cigarettes and just as many when there was a cigarette shortage! Non-smokers, such as Alan Moore, were able to use cigarettes as bargaining tools to exchange for food or other items which they wanted. In the same way, food from Red Cross parcels could be 'exchanged' between the men to satisfy particular tastes:

gave Moore jam for cheese.

Dad also had notes in his diary which appear to be 'accounts' for money owed for the purchase of various items from friends;

Oct 20th	From A Moore for cigs and tobacco	21pf
Oct 25th	From A Moore for bread and tobacco	27pf
	From A Moore for bread	2
	From A Dey for honey	7
Dec 28th	From A Moore for fags	14
Jan 14th 1941	PAID A MOORE	70pf
	Paid A Dey	7

All dues it seems, were paid in full!

Sunday 24th November 1940
No work - no service – sausage & pork pies for tea – got buckshee soup –concert at night – sausage & dripping

Tuesday 26th November 1940
Got separated from river party today – working in wood yard (sawing wood) – our section had buckshee soup today – sausage & dripping. Got shirt and sox – biscuit issue

Wednesday 27th November 1940
Work on river again – one of coldest days yet – finished very late – cheese & dripping issue

Along with obtaining 'buckshees' was the art of 'fiddling' items of food. We are not entirely sure what this involved but it seems to have been a fairly common practice!

Alistair also noted that on 26 November Forster made a speech in Graudenz. This must have been the notorious Albert Forster, Gauleiter of the Reichsgau Danzig West whose objective was the total Germanisation of the entire region. He was later sentenced to death for his war crimes.[11]

Thursday 28th November 1940
Work on river again - I fiddled 18 rolls (guard took three) - Alistair fiddled pkts of Fumona, 3 pkts cig papers, 5 boxes of matches and cucumbers (guard searched everybody) - very cold again - sausage & dripping issue. A little snow tonight

Fumona was a type of locally grown tobacco and is mentioned frequently as were Junaks, a brand of German cigarette produced in occupied Poland during the war for Polish citizens.

The German guards were fully aware that POWs tried to smuggle food and tobacco back into camp, hence the regular searches. Sometimes they would turn a blind eye, but they could cause a big upset by conducting searches and confiscating the items found.

Alan Moore had been in hospital with bad circulation since the start of the month but was back with the others again by the end of November. Dad, it seems, was keeping well despite the worsening weather, as stated in his own words, 'first real touch of winter on Friday & Saturday'.

On the first day of December, a Sunday, Dad was issued with 60 Junaks and a pair of hand mitts! Later that month another blanket was issued. As the winter weather became more severe any extra items made a huge difference. According to Alistair's account, it became so cold later in the month that the river froze, and temperatures dropped to minus 15 degrees Celsius.

Monday 2nd December 1940
Work on river – Alistair in woodyard – we finished at 1 o'clock – jam & sausage – got letter from Mother and Mrs James dated 4th September – good news – received my cards at home

Dad must have been very relieved to know that those at home in Scotland had received his cards and knew that he was well. The importance of receiving mail from home could never be underestimated and the disappointment was acute for those who did not receive any letters when mail was distributed at the camp. Dad was generally lucky in receiving regular post as his mother was a conscientious letter writer but on occasion he was without any;

some mail received today - no luck!!

Friday 6th December 1940
Three of us working in wood yard today – no bread – sausage & dripping issue

Saturday 7th December 1940
Work on river – very cold – sausage & dripping issue

The cold winter weather continued, and Dad hoped the river job was finally coming to an end:

Very cold indeed this last week - strong rumour that river job ends on Monday first - hope so!!!!

However, up until his final diary entry on 11 December, he was still working on the river.

Monday 9th December 1940
Work on river – finished part of river – much milder today. A Moore went to work in wood yard – sausage & dripping issue

Tuesday 10th December 1940
Work on river – party of 20 – fiddled 2 pkts biscuits – Alistair one jam sandwich, Archie ditto – finished 12 o'clock

Wednesday 11th December 1940
Work on river party of 20 – jam sandwich each – International Red Cross issue 3 Ovo Sports cake [OVO Sports was a kind of biscuit bar made with Ovaltine] chocolate, 3 cheeses, 4 extract cubes, tin of jam between four, tin meat between 2 – dripping & crowdie issue'

Dad had now been in captivity for six months. Diary pages for the remainder of December were torn out but there was a note listing the contents of a Red Cross parcel for 30 December 1940:

1\4 lb Cadbury's Milk Choc, 1\4 lb Tea, Pkt Sugar, 1 Bar Soap, Tin Yeatex (a type of yeast extract), 3 Tins Chicken & Ham Roll, Tin Haricot Oxtail, Tin Veg & Gravy, Tin Tomato Juice, Box Cheese, Tin Milk Powder, Tin Beef Dripping, Tin Honey, Tin Salmon, Tin Peas.

This was significant as, unusually, the men all received one Red Cross parcel per man on this occasion!

The only other entry relating to 1940 was an account written up on separate pieces of paper of which Dad had composed two slightly different versions. 'The Wrong Xmas Spirit' tells of an incident that took place at Graudenz on Christmas Eve. Some POWs had managed to get out of the camp and were caught when they were returning with 'buckshees'.

One of Dad's accounts is reproduced below. It is possible that this was written after his return home as he was very careful not to mention anything in his diaries which could get him into trouble if discovered.

It is midnight Xmas Eve 1940. Forgetful of the intensely bitter cold, we stand half clothed and shivering, witnessing a spectacle which must be unique even in a POW camp in Poland. Moved by gnawing pangs of hunger, some of the 'Tommies' scale the 20 feet of barbed wire. Fate decrees that a watchful guard should espy the last returning adventurer. We disappear within the billets like smoke, but as quickly we are 'clubbed' on parade by rifle butts. Three colleagues are picked at random and face Nazi guards armed with machine guns, who are instructed to shoot within two minutes if the miscreants fail to step forward. Two seconds is long enough to test the British Spirit. The leering Commandant's,

'Remember remember
The 24th of December'
rings in my ears yet. The wages of desperation are reduced rations on Xmas Day. But fate decrees strange results!

Alistair also recalls this event, and, in his version, we learn that a soldier did in fact step forward before any shots were fired. Everyone expected the worst to happen, but the Commandant unexpectedly shook the soldier's hand and called him a brave man! The situation was luckily defused without serious incident.

'........ some daring spirits endeavoured to climb the wire to contact the Poles for food. This was doomed to failure and at a roll call in the darkness the Commandant demanded to know who were involved. If no one owned up he intended to shoot several of us picked at random. Knowing him, anything was possible. Silence can be inexplicably long and after repeated threats a small soldier stepped forward. Expecting the worst, we held our breath until the mercurial Commandant shook him by the hand, called him a brave man and dismissed the parade with the admonition "Remember, remember, ..."

In a separate entry Alistair also writes:

'Christmas Eve, some boys outside at night. Got past guard at gate then through wire. Came back loaded with bucks. Shows quite easy to escape. Gerry still mad over last night's escapade. Kept everyone on their toes. 2 who were caught by police going to Stalag. Other 11 working at barbed wire fence.'[12]

The tension-filled midnight roll call had ended peacefully and without any shots being fired, but the Commandant decided that punishment was still due. On Christmas Day therefore all POWs were denied any extra privileges, already meagre rations were reduced and all day they were made to carry out monotonous duties in and around the camp. Dad wrote:

And on the 25th the already meagre rations are cut - no bread issue - and oh what heavenly delight for just one puff of a cig. But Dame Fortune DOES smile again!

Alistair also noted:

'25th Christmas Day. Kept on hop all day – cleaning and recleaning room. Only extra, more spuds in soup! NO mail – nothing. Drip & saus. No concert.'[13]

As the new year came around Dad's diary entries resumed. The men were already back out working and it seems that at long last the river detail had come to an end.

Thursday 2nd January 1941
Working on foundation job – made fire and stood by it all day – dripping and sausage

The weather remained bitterly cold but, although still working outdoors, there was at least now an opportunity to build a fire in order to keep warm.

Friday 3rd January 1941
*Working on foundation job again – Archie & Alistair
in sand pits – made fire again – very cold – had milk in
coffee at night – we protested – dripping and sausage –
mended blinds*

Saturday 4th January 1941
*No work – our company deloused – tin condensed milk
issued (delicious) – jam & crowdie issue*

Sunday 5th January 1941
*No work – no service – inspected by Major Duffus for new
battledress and boots – sausage & dripping*

Major Duffus is first mentioned by Alistair in December 1940:

'100 men from Stalag – Major Duffus as MO! Had talk
with Maj D – issue of 2 razor blades'[14]

His name comes up a number of times between the months of
January and March in both Dad's and Alistair's recollections. We got
the impression that they both had met him previously.

On Saturday 18th January Dad writes:

….. inspected by Duffus again – diphtheria

Article 15 of *The Geneva Convention* states that 'medical inspections
of POWs shall be arranged once a month' [15] and amongst other things
specifies the detection of infectious diseases. Although there were
cases of diphtheria at Stalag XXA, any spread was quickly contained
by programmes of vaccinations supplied by the ICRC. Dad's POW
records show he was vaccinated against diphtheria in December 1940
and on 18 January 1941. The following year he received a typhus
inoculation. Any typhus epidemics were also quickly arrested and
both the medical personnel and most of the POWs were vaccinated
against it. Regular disinfection took place to try and eliminate vermin,
fleas and bugs and rooms or even whole huts were set aside for

delousing. It was indicated in *The International Committee of the Red Cross Report* that conditions such as TB, ulcers, gastritis and nephritis were noted. In addition, cases of Furunculosis, or boils, were common.[16]

Towards the end of March Alistair writes:

'22 March 1941: Duffus going to Stalag (Fort 13A)

25 March 1941: Duffus left at 05.15' [17]

This was Major G M Rae Duffus[18] who was a doctor in general practice in Aberdeen both before and after the war. In 1938 he became a member of the RAMC (TA) with the 153 Field Ambulance attached to the 51st Highland Division and was sent to France in January 1940 with the rest of the Division. After capture at St Valery-en-Caux he was initially taken to Oflag VIIC at Laufen in Bavaria then in December 1940 he was moved to Stalag XXA as Medical Officer. We understand that Major Duffus carried out inspections in many of the work camps, including Graudenz and Stalag XXA at Thorn and from the diary notes we can tell that he was at Graudenz from the end of December 1940 until March 1941. A year later, in March 1942 he was moved to Stalag XXB at Marienburg where he became Senior Medical Officer. Marienburg (now Malbork) was similar to Thorn in that the main camp was an administration centre with most of the prisoners based elsewhere on work parties, sometimes as much as one hundred miles away.

We have since met with Major Duffus's son Peter who gave us some interesting information about his father's role within the 153 Field Ambulance. It turns out that he was also at Crookham in late 1939 so it might be that Dad and Alistair remembered him from those early days. Major Duffus may even have provided some of the training for the men at this time.

In the early days of January, the continuing bitterly cold weather prompted both Dad and Alistair to report sick with flu resulting in a couple of days' reprieve inside the camp.

9. Major Rae Duffus in Captain's uniform. Reproduced by kind permission of Peter Duffus.

Monday 6th January 1941
Working on dump unloading carts of snow – Alistair sick (flu) – bought 60pf loaf and two 30pf's from Pole – new lot of 100 men arrived – sausage and dripping

Tuesday 7th January 1941
Reported sick – touch of flu – got 2 days off work – PARCEL arrived from HOME – wrote PC's home

Despite being sick, both Alistair and Dad were kept busy 'on spuds' which we assume meant peeling potatoes for the camp kitchen.

Wednesday 8th January 1941
*Alistair and I on spuds – Archie fiddled loaf and 'Tongas' –
issue of tins of fruit*

Tongas were German cigarettes made in Graudenz itself.

Even while confined to the camp, opportunities could still arise to obtain extra food – *bought some bread from Polish electrician in camp – still on spuds*

Friday 10th January 1941
*Still sick - Red Cross parcel per man - got 5 letters from
mother (last one dated 25th Nov) - Archie working in MI
room.*

Receiving mail from home was still greatly anticipated, even when the news was from weeks before.

By the start of the following week Dad was well enough to be sent back out to work.

Monday 13th January 1941
*Back to work – bought 2 pkts of 'Tongas' on woodyard –
Alistair still in sick bay*

Tuesday 14th January 1941
*On roads today shifting snow – Alistair came out of sick
bay – got paid 4 marks 70 pfennigs*

Wednesday 15th January 1941
*Archie & Alistair both sick – working on roads sweeping
snow – fiddled piece bread and one pound fresh butter*

The work details for January were mainly related to the wintry conditions - apart from a few days in the woodyard Dad was either on the roads shifting snow or working at the snow dump.

Saturday 18th January 1941
*Working in woodyard again – some mail arrived – Archie
got 2 Xmas cards and 2 letters – Alistair has had no mail
so far.*

It must have been very disheartening for Alistair to have received no mail for eight months, especially as his two close friends were getting regular batches of letters as well as parcels of clothing and books.

Sunday 19th January 1941
No work – no service – received parcel of 4 books from Mother – concert at night

A note for the same date in Alistair's memoirs refers to Dad having received a parcel of books and that he (Alistair) was reading one of them. The friends shared whatever they had with one another whether it was food they had fiddled or books they received from home. They truly helped one another through these hardest of times.

Most of the outdoor work at this time was related to the winter weather but sometimes it was too cold even to shift snow and the men were kept indoors.

Wednesday 22nd January 1941
Archie indoors for new boots – snow shifting again – shirts and socks issued

Thursday 23rd January 1941
Archie and I on the snow dump – bought 60 pf loaf, tobacco & papers – got buckshee loaf from guard – got issued with another blanket – bought 100 Junaks

Monday 27th January 1941
Snow shifting – extremely cold (-25 degrees F) – lots of cases of frostbite – got 5 letters from Mother and one from Arthur

Tuesday 28th January 1941
'Nix arbeit' [meaning 'no work'] – extremely cold (about 20 below) – issued with Red Cross Parcel today

Wednesday 29th January 1941
No work – extremely cold – reading all day – all issued

with clogs – wrote letter cards home

We remember Dad telling us about having to wear wooden clogs during the winter months and how they would wrap cloths around their feet to try to keep them warm and dry.

He received a lot of letters during this month as well as a clothing parcel and a book parcel - five letters from his mother on the 10th, a parcel of four books from his mother on the 19th, eleven letters (eight of which were from his mother) on the 20th, a letter and Christmas card from his mother on the 25th and a further three letters on the 30th!

February remained bitterly cold for the most part. Dad was still being asked to carry out a lot of hard, manual labour - mainly sweeping snow, picking ice (in Adolf Hitler Strasse), clearing slush and working on the snow dump. On occasion this was relieved by spells of labour in the woodyard, shovelling 'ground' on the riverbank, working in the cement yard and shifting bricks as well as demolition and foundation jobs. Opportunities for fiddling extras still arose of course, sometimes in the most unlikely of places!

Friday 14th February 1941
On snow dump – bought 3 30pf loaves – fiddled pkt of cigs in latrine, some tobacco, sandwich – woman bought 2 60pf loaves for the party – got 5 letters from Mother, Xmas card from Jean, letter from Milly and letter from Mrs James

On a couple of occasions Dad mentions the luxury of having a bath;

...had usual weekly bath today...

and another time 'a hot spray'.

POWs hired out to military and civilian contractors were supposed to receive pay and this was usually in the form of 'camp money' or 'lagergeld' which could only be used in the canteens or shops set up for the prisoners. They could exchange the 'lagergeld' for basic items such as a toothbrush, toothpaste and boot polish. Sometimes welcome extras such as bread, sweets, biscuits and cigarettes were available and eventually small diaries stamped with 'Stalag XXA' could also be purchased, one of which Dad used for writing his later notes.

10. Example of camp money or 'lagergeld'.

On several occasions during the early months of 1941, Dad talks of buying lemonade or even beer from the camp canteen.

Saturday 15th February 1941
Picking ice on roads – long day – bottle beer each at night – flogged stew for 2 Jerry loaves

Saturday 22nd February 1941
On roads picking ice – wet, cold & muddy – fiddled fruit cake – got 2 letters from Mother 13th & 15th January - got paid 19 marks - bottle beer each

Wednesday 26th February 1941
On demolishing job – cold & snowing – bottle lemonade each at night – got 29 Marks 50pf RAMC money

Dad writes that he received RAMC pay in February and notes again on 28 March: got paid 30 marks (RAMC)

Friday 28th February 1941
Went sick today – made pancakes – received letter from

*Mother & Harry – had 3 bottles beer & bottle lemonade –
bought cig papers*

A day off 'sick' gave Dad the opportunity to make pancakes!

His last mention of buying beer or lemonade was towards the end of April:

*Work again – cold today – new guards – got second
clothing parcel from Mother – Archie got parcel also –
lemonade tonight*

Again, Dad was fortunate to receive quite a number of letters this month - nineteen in all, mostly from his mother but also from his sisters Jean and Milly and other family members. Alistair however, had still not received any mail since his capture eight months before and on 5 February he writes:

'Visit from Red Cross rep. Told parcels regular now. Names taken of those who have had no mail. Cable will be sent from Geneva and reply delivered to person in question.' [19]

Alistair did however receive indirect news from home as our grandmother Amelia kept in touch with both Alistair's and Archie's families and related news from them via her letters to Dad. Alistair writes:

'In Allan's letter, Dad wrote to his mother, had received a letter card'

'Word of home per Allan's letters'

'Mail for Allan and Archie - none for me! By their letters Dad had 3 from me dated Dec & Jan' [20]

Finally, in May 1941 Alistair received a backlog of twenty-three letters!

During the month of February, they were pleased to receive Red Cross food and clothing parcels and further International Red Cross issues.

Monday 24th February 1941
Working on snow dump – snowed all day – got Red Cross khaki shirt and pants

Tuesday 25th January 1941
Snow sweeping on roads – fiddled buns and cigs – Red Cross Parcel each

Throughout February Dad continues to be involved in clearing snow but in March he mentions being out on foundation jobs, ditch digging and working on 'barracks jobs' at various locations - 'Jerry barracks, Berwinsok St Barracks, Pioneer Barracks.' This afforded him and his friends the usual opportunities to fiddle extra food.

Thursday 6th March 1941
On barrack job again – fiddled loaf – got 200 Players from Mother

Friday 7th March 1941
On Jerry barracks – fiddled loaf. Archie on corporation job – got dinner on job

Saturday 8th March 1941
On Berwinsok St Barracks – fiddled bread, tin meat & sausages

During March he writes that he had a tooth filled by the dentist, was deloused and also reported sick. He mentions writing a postcard to France and we think this might have been to one of the girls he met during the days of the Phoney War in early 1940!

On 27 March he writes that a huge search of the camp was carried out by the German guards although he does not say what triggered it. We were very surprised to read what items were uncovered!

Jerries made thorough search of the whole camp - found amazing amount of bread, maps, Jerry money, guns, wireless, axe, compass etc. Archie managed to save our 'brot' [bread]

Around this time, we learned from notes that Alistair made that there was considerable unrest among the local Polish population and that German soldiers had been killed.

Just as the month of March drew to a close there was a big change in routine. On Sunday 30 March Dad received word that he was to be transferred to a different Company and on the following day was sent on a two-hour train journey to the town of Laskowitz (now called Laskowice):

Monday 31st March 1941
New job today – went to Laskowitz by train – digging trench for cable – 1/5 loaf each

Nine

Selkirk

April to September 2012

As the river Vistula made its way from the Beskidy Mountains towards the Baltic Sea it swept past Graudenz where Dad and his fellow inmates had just spent their first nine months in captivity. It had been a harsh winter and a time of hard labour and food shortages. The monotonous routine of camp life was reflected in Dad's writing. 'Ditto,' was often the only comment written for four or five consecutive days.

We had now completed the transcription of the first of his three diaries, but it was his last one which we were curious about. It had 'Stalag XXA' stamped in gold-coloured lettering on its cover and German print inside. While in captivity our father had kept a record of all his correspondence and as we skimmed through the pages, we noticed that the name Kathleen Tait appeared in some of his entries.

> *Warm - had two letters from Mother & one from Kathleen Tait - wrote PC to Mother, Mrs Sutherland & Madame Lensel France.*

> 9th July 1942

Kathleen Tait was a name we recognised from conversations with our aunt Jean when she reminisced about her younger days and from her we discovered that Kathleen had been a colleague of Dad's at the Inverness solicitors and had known the Cameron family well. We were aware of a Kathleen Dunlop who lived locally but did not know her personally. Yet we had an inkling that she may well be the person our father mentioned in his diaries. Weeks later, a chance meeting with one of Kathleen's family confirmed that Tait was indeed her maiden name and we were delighted to hear that she wanted to meet up with us.

Although now in her 90s, she had a keen memory and had many stories to tell about life in Inverness and Nairn during and after the war. We heard about Kathleen's time at the solicitors and we were able to show her Dad's original indenture form for which she had been a signatory in June 1938. We were pleased when our visit turned out to be the first of many fascinating afternoon chats.

It was now four months since we had sent a message to Alistair's son Stuart MacRitchie and we had not yet heard back. We felt sure that Stuart and George, his brother, would be keen to know that we were now in touch with Alan, an ex-POW who had known their father well in Stalag XXA and the challenge was now to try and find an alternative way of making contact.

We had a feeling that George had possibly lived and worked in the Glasgow area some years ago, but we had no current address or contact details. From the book-publishing website we learned that Stuart had recently retired after working for a large Canadian company, but further searches came up with no new information. It seemed that we had reached a dead end.

It was not until late one March evening that we had a breakthrough. While browsing on the internet it occurred to us that Stuart could well be part of a well-known online community that focuses on developing professional networking. Good fortune and luck were on our side as a quick search confirmed that Stuart was indeed a member and could be contacted directly by email. As we were not members ourselves, a brief message was forwarded by Laura on our behalf explaining that she was the granddaughter of Allan Cameron whom their father (Alistair MacRitchie) had known during the war.

We were cautiously optimistic but thought no more about it until the next morning when an unexpected reply came through from a very surprised Stuart. We were equally surprised and delighted! It transpired that our original message had never reached Stuart and he had no idea that we had tried to contact him several months previously.

E-mails quickly followed. There were family memories, stories of our fathers' wartime experiences and recollections of Dad's and Alistair's friendship after the war to talk about. We were now in touch with George too and, of course, there was the good news about Alan Moore to share.

After explaining that a meeting with Alan and Hilda had been planned for the summer, we discovered that, by chance, Stuart and his wife Velma had already booked flights to Glasgow in September. There was now the distinct possibility that we could co-ordinate a visit for all of us to meet up together.

A quick phone call alerted Alan and Hilda to the latest development. They were delighted to hear that Alistair's family had been contacted and it turned out that meeting up sometime in September suited them too. Addresses and e-mails were shared and the business of arranging a date and place began to take shape.

Unfortunately, no information about Archie or his family, if he had any, had surfaced. However, not long after hearing from Stuart, Fiona had a clear out of paperwork and came across an old forgotten address book of Dad's which contained Archie's name, telephone number and an address in Irvine. Trying the phone number, we were surprised when someone answered. However, the present occupiers, who had lived in the house for the past twenty years, had no knowledge of the Dey family. A further enquiry to the Irvine British Legion Association also drew a blank.

In late spring we were pleased to hear from George MacRitchie. He and his wife Linda were visiting the Inverness area, so we made an arrangement to meet them for lunch. There was plenty to catch up on.

After over fifty years it was refreshing to talk about our time in Glasgow and to share what we knew about Dad's and Alistair's past. Our hope now was that everything would go to plan for our September meeting with Alan and Hilda. Five months still seemed a very long time away.

September 2012

The arrangements for our meeting all fell into place and on 21 September 2012 we boarded the early train from Inverness to travel south. Watching the scenery slip by we were reminded of Dad's description of 'purple-clad hills in their rock studded heathery garments' which he had written in an essay some years after the war. Our father should have been making this journey...not us.

> 'Dad...would you believe it! Tomorrow we'll be meeting up with Alan Moore...from Stalag XXA...along with Alistair's family... George and Stuart MacRitchie. It's difficult to put into words the mixed feelings we have after such a remarkable few months.'

A year ago, our intention had been simply to make a transcript of Dad's diaries but fate or 'Dame Fortune,' as our father might have said, was to change all that. Whatever the reasons for the coincidences, the twists and turns that connected the Highlands to Glasgow, Yorkshire and Canada came about within a space of less than six months.

The lucky timing of the discovery of the diaries, Alistair's memoirs and Alan's appearance on the BBC had been a remarkable stroke of good fortune. After the broadcast Alan had been contacted by many relatives of veterans who had been in Stalag XXA, but it turned out that our father was the only POW whom he had personally known from that time.

By early summer we had completed transcribing Dad's notebooks and sent copies to Stuart, George and Alan. When Alan phoned to thank us, he said it 'brought tears to his eyes.' The diaries, it seemed, reflected what life had been like as a POW. Even what was left unsaid told a story. For us, there was also no doubt that the voice that had spoken to us from the pages was the person we had always known.

Arriving in Edinburgh we mingled with shoppers and tourists as we made our way towards the bus station in St Andrew's Square. Our destination was the historic town of Selkirk and arriving a day early to fit in with travel times gave us an ideal opportunity to meet up with Alan and Hilda for afternoon tea.

The quiet lounge in the picturesque Glen Hotel was the ideal venue and it was a delight to meet Alan and Hilda in person. They were interesting and entertaining company and their fondness for, and knowledge of, Scotland combined with our own family connections, and holidays in the Yorkshire area meant we had plenty to talk about. We did not discuss the war years - that was on the agenda for tomorrow.

Alan's Day

The next morning Stuart and Velma arrived at the hotel. George and Linda were on their way. This was the first time we had seen Stuart since we were children but there was little time to reminisce. It was Alan's day.

That morning Alan described his experiences clearly and eloquently as we heard his extraordinary account of what he had witnessed. Like many others Alan's story had remained untold for years and it was only when he reached his 70s that he had begun to speak about his past. Although some of Alan's memories of life as a POW appear later in the story what follows is an account of most of what we heard that day.

All four men had been in the 153 FA as part of the RAMC. As Alan was from Sunderland, it was at Newbattle Abbey, Dalkeith, where he was enlisted as a hospital cook and completed his army training. On leaving school he had trained as a confectioner, chocolatier and baker and although he had no cooking experience the army decided that it was a hospital cook he was going to be.

After only six weeks of basic army training Alan was sent to France. Initially he had been assigned to the 154 FA but after four weeks he asked for a transfer to join the 153 FA to be alongside a friend. His request was granted and Alan was sent to help at the casualty clearing stations in the Alsace region. It was here that Alan thought he may have briefly met Dad, Alistair and Archie.

11. Private Alan Moore. By kind permission of Alan Moore.

111

Weeks later Alan was also captured on the 12th June at St Valery-en-Caux. While Dad, Alistair and Archie had been making their way to St Valery-en-Caux from the south, Alan had been travelling with convoys along the coast taking casualties from the north to a hospital in the town.

Before capture those in the 153 and 152 FAs had been ordered directly by the British government to stay in France to look after the dying and wounded. Anyone from those units who was found back in the UK faced being court-martialled and risked being 'shot'. Any written material which could give information to the enemy had also to be destroyed. Alan felt the troops seemed ill prepared for battle as they had out-dated equipment and many of the rules from the First World War were still being applied. For the FA, who were unarmed, 'bandages were their ammunition.'

Alan too had witnessed the loss of life at St Valery-en-Caux and he was one of the many who had tried to clamber down the cliffs by using makeshift ropes in an attempt to escape. Many were shot but Alan believed that wearing his Red Cross armband had saved his life that day.

When the 51st surrendered, Alan also became one of the thousands who marched out of St Valery-en-Caux as a POW. He recalled that the line of captured soldiers was two miles long and seven men wide and he remembered the harsh conditions and treatment they had to endure on the journey across northern Europe to Poland. Alan vividly remembered being pulled out of line with other POWs, marched into a nearby wooded area and threatened at gunpoint by guards. This 'mock execution' was purely for the amusement of the guards and on this occasion, no one was shot.

When they reached Holland, they travelled on coal barges and although Alan tried to see the funny side of ending up blackened by coal dust it was also a grim experience. Once in Germany, cattle trucks used as transport had only standing room, no sanitation and men were known to have died on the journey. It was when he eventually arrived at Stalag XXA that Alan clearly recalled meeting Dad, Alistair and Archie.

At the camp in Graudenz where they were first sent to work Alan said they were treated as 'slave labour.' Men collapsed with exhaustion due to hard physical work and lack of adequate food. According to the Geneva Convention those in the RAMC should not have had to do heavy manual labour but they had no choice and Alan still felt strongly about this injustice. We heard that Dad, Alistair and Archie were inseparable at this time and were known as 'the three twins' by their fellow inmates!

In the camps, conditions were often not what they seemed. When blankets were eventually distributed, they turned out to be paper thin and 'useless' for their intended purpose. Issue soap consisted of sand, gelatine and glycerine and clothes taken from other POWs were often handed out to British prisoners by the German guards.

After many months of hard manual labour Alan eventually became the hospital cook at Fort XIV, Stalag XXA. There was so little food that the soup made in the camp kitchens was ninety per cent water. Making the most of what was available was vital and when Alan was once given a barrel of herring, he made his own version of 'fish and chips.' He recalled that the German guards asked him to prepare some for them too!

The hospital was only for the most serious cases and could only accommodate one hundred patients. It became so overcrowded that at one point they had to erect wooden huts on the roof and Alan recalled that some patients, in desperation, attempted to jump.

It was while at Fort XIV that Alan managed to acquire his radio from the Polish resistance. We heard more about the dangers he had faced to smuggle it into the camp in exchange for a hundred cigarettes hidden under a corpse.

Listening to the radio was risky and a look-out always had to be around when it was in use. Alan tuned in to the BBC news whenever possible but had to be careful when passing on information from the broadcasts. Not everyone could be trusted.

Towards the end of 1943 Alan had the chance to be repatriated but a friend begged Alan to give him his place. His wife had left home and his parents were looking after their two young children. Alan sought advice from a higher-ranking POW and although told in no uncertain terms that when the war ended it would be a messy affair, he eventually agreed to give up his chance of returning to the UK. After the war Alan learned that the friend who had taken his place had joined the paratroopers on his return but had sadly died at Arnhem.

After Alan had given up the chance of returning to the UK, conditions for the POWs took a turn for the worse. As the Russians were advancing, the Germans pulled back westwards and British POWs were sent to a camp twenty miles from Thorn called Kopernicus. During the shift from Stalag XXA Alan managed to take his radio with him by hiding it inside a packing box. Food was again in short supply and at one point Alan weighed only seven stone.

Alan eventually escaped from Kopernicus with the help of a doctor while working as a stretcher bearer. He fled across the frozen Vistula only to be captured by the Russian army in nearby forests. Escaping once more he made his way to Warsaw where, with the help of Polish partisans, he hid in the sewers before again being arrested by the Russians. Alan was then sent to prison in Odessa. While there he befriended a female German spy whom he helped to avoid detection.

It was in Odessa that Alan witnessed the tragic fate of 'White' Russians who were returning to the USSR by ship under the terms of the Yalta agreement. Fearing what would happen to them many jumped from the ship in sight of the dock. The remaining men, women and children who were taken from the vessel were lined up on the quayside and shot by Russian troops. Alan and the other Allied prisoners were then made to board this same ship to be returned to the UK. This episode, which had been kept a closely guarded secret for decades, was Alan's most traumatic memory of the war. To this day it still haunts him.

As we all sat together around the table we were surprised when Alan brought out the radio which had featured on the Remembrance Special programme. It was extraordinary to hear that it had been hidden and kept secret from his captors for so long before surviving the journey from Poland via Odessa to the UK. It was even more remarkable to learn that the bulky receiver had avoided detection by being sewn into the lining of Alan's coat. He told us that he filled the pocket on the opposite side to balance up the weight of the radio using bars of chocolate which had been melted together with dried fruits.

After lunch we had time to ask questions and to look through the memorabilia we had all brought along. Stuart and George had taken Alistair's sizeable collection of documents and paperwork from the war era and while looking through one of his diaries it randomly fell open at a page where Alistair had written, 'Allan gets glasses.' From Dad's assortment of artefacts, we were able to produce the very replacement glasses that Alistair was referring to!

Along with photos and paperwork, we had decided at the last minute to take along an old army jacket of our father's. We were interested to find out more about its origins as it did not match descriptions of British Army issue uniforms. The only clue was its 'Nonpareil' label. Alan explained to us that the jacket had probably been taken from another prisoner by the German guards and as often happened, was then re-issued. But it was Dad's POW number written in black indelible ink on the inside of the collar that caught Alan's attention.

 Dad's number was 18476 and Alan's POW number was only one digit higher. Alan realised that he must have been standing in line behind our father in July 1940 when they were officially registered as prisoners at Stalag XXA. There were many questions still to ask Alan about the war, but we were also curious to know if he had ever met up with Dad, Alistair or Archie on his return to the UK.

After the war Alan had a very successful business career in the food industry and on two occasions had lived and worked in Scotland. When time allowed Alan and Hilda had travelled extensively around the country. On one trip to the West Coast they had visited Alistair's hometown of Fort William. While there Alan made enquiries about Alistair but unfortunately no one he spoke to was able to give him information about the MacRitchie family or their whereabouts. Yet, on another occasion it turned out to be a chance meeting during the

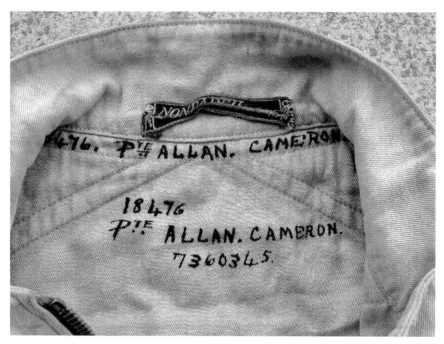

12. Jacket belonging to Dad with POW number written inside collar.

'50s or early '60s that was to once again remind Alan of his time as a POW.

It was in either Manchester or Glasgow, when, out of the blue, Alan and Dad unexpectedly bumped into each other. Although Alan could not recall whether it was at a business meeting or in the street, he clearly remembered that they greeted each other with a hug, exchanged phone numbers and promised to get in touch.

Not long afterwards Alan moved to the south of England, our father relocated north and the opportunity for them to get together was lost. Looking back now Alan deeply regretted that he, Dad, Alistair, and Archie had not taken the opportunity to meet up forty years ago.

We left Selkirk with many questions answered and a more vivid understanding of the experiences of those who had been captured at St Valery-en-Caux and held in captivity. Most of all it had been a privilege to meet Alan and to hear him describe with remarkable detail and clarity his personal account of the war. His survival of capture, years of imprisonment, escape and hardship was testament to his extraordinary bravery, self-sacrifice and determination. It was a day that we would never forget.

Before leaving a last minute group photograph was taken.

13. Selkirk meeting. Back row, from left: Stuart MacRitchie, Velma MacRitchie, Carole Grant, Fiona Cameron, Linda MacRitchie, George MacRitchie. Front row, from left: Hilda Moore, Alan Moore.

Ten

How Much Longer Now?

April 1941 to March 1943

Monday 31st March 1941
*New job today – went to Laskowitz by train – digging
trench for cable – 1/5 loaf each*

Dad's new work detail was in a neighbouring village called Laskowitz (now known as Laskowice Pomorskie), a major rail junction about 13 miles away from Graudenz. Although not always working alongside our father, Alan was also part of this labour party and he recalls the daily train journey in cattle rail wagons. As far as we know the men returned to the camp at Graudenz each evening.

The job in Laskowitz involved digging trenches for laying cables. This was extremely hard physical work which led to many of the POWs becoming totally exhausted. According to Alan they were given little more to eat than a portion of mouldy loaf each day. He also told us that he believed that the cables being laid in the trenches were for the German electrical manufacturing company Siemens. Each five-metre stretch of trench had to be one-metre-deep and half a metre wide. He also explained that there were rumours and some unease about the eventual purpose of the cables being laid and even the guards were unhappy about this work, becoming annoyed when any of the men accidently slipped into the trenches.

Alan vividly recalled one particular day when he became very weak and unwell whilst working. He had lost a lot of weight as a result of poor diet and hard work and eventually collapsed. He was lifted out of the way and then left lying on the cold ground, unaided. Alan told us he felt sure he would have died that day had an army doctor (either a German or an Austrian) not noticed him and ordered his transfer back to camp to be given medical treatment and good food to bring him back to health. Later, when he was recovering in the hospital, Alan asked this same doctor why he had taken the trouble to help him. The reply was that he was repaying a favour from a time when he had been shot in the arm during World War One. When his wound had started to become gangrenous, he explained that a British doctor took care of him and helped him recover fully. He was sure that he owed his life to this man and felt that by helping Alan he had found a way of repaying his debt.

Thursday 10th April 1941
Laid cables – warm today – wrote letter to Mother and PC to Mrs James

Dad spent at least the first half of the month digging trenches and laying cables although they were all given a day's holiday for Easter on the fourteenth;

No work today – Easter holiday

A change of guards meant another day off on the twenty-first and he also spent a day here and there indoors trying to sort out new glasses:

Tuesday 15th April 1941
Not out today – waited to see Jerry doctor about new glasses but he did not come

Friday 18th April 1941

.... got my eyes tested for new glasses at opticians in town....
new specs due in a fortnight

It was not until the first week in May however that he eventually received them.

Friday 2nd May 1941

Stayed in today to get new glasses but they were not ready –
cheery bloke in opticians – try again Monday

Monday 5th May 1941

Stayed in today –got new glasses at opticians – company
came back early today due to heavy rain

Dad kept these glasses and brought them back home with him.

14. *Dad's glasses with case. Inside case is a note giving his base address as Fort XIV*
and details of his prescription.

Both the glasses and his prescription were perfectly intact inside a metal case labelled 'Dienst-Brille' [service glasses].

By now most POWs were adept at bartering with the Poles and were able to acquire many useful items including radio sets. This vital link to the outside world helped keep them informed about what was happening at home in the UK, throughout Europe and further afield during the long months and years of their incarceration.

Perhaps by this means Dad learned about the fall of Greece. On 28 April he writes in his diary:

Did Greece fall about now?

Greece did indeed surrender on 27 April 1941.

Our father had now been in Graudenz for nine months and he and his close friends Archie, Alistair and Alan Moore were still together.

Dad's daily work routine was still monotonous, and the weather remained cold and snowy right into the month of May. He must have had some trouble with his teeth as there were a number of visits to the camp dentist during this month. Dad notes that Archie also received dental treatment.

Thursday 8th May 1941
Cold, snow & sleet – went to dentist again & got tooth filled

There was mention of an escape attempt at this time too and of the recapture of a former escapee:

Tuesday 6th May 1941
*Benny & Weeks made their escape today – sergeant in
4 company was recaptured at Frankfurt on train after a
fortnight's freedom*

Wednesday 7th May 1941
*- guards discovered that Benny & Weeks were missing -
they conducted a futile search in the Polish houses opposite
the camp*

However, news on 12 May hit much closer to home:

Work today – as I write this in the train it is a glorious morning – warm & sunny - big development when we arrived back tonight - Alistair goes to Stalag tomorrow.

Having been together for so long, it came as a big disappointment for Dad to discover that Alistair had been detailed to join a new work party and would now be separated from his friends.

Alistair left for Stalag this morning - gave him socks, jersey, camp money - I sincerely hope we meet again soon

A couple of days later our Dad received news:

.. got a note from Alistair at Fort 13A - lousy dump

Alistair managed to find a way of contacting Dad on his arrival at Fort 13A. He wrote a note for our father which he then passed to one of the POWs who was also at Stalag XXA collecting canteen stock to take back to Graudenz. The POW then passed Alistair's note on to Dad.

There were no further diary entries for 1941 but from our father's German POW record card we know that he left Graudenz in August of 1941 and returned to Stalag XXA at Thorn. By this time Alistair had been moved away from Thorn to Schlüsselmühle on a new work detail.

Alan Moore told us that that the trench digging and cable laying work lasted for about nine months in total, so it is likely that Dad continued on this work detail from May until he left Graudenz in August. Although we don't know if Archie returned to Thorn at the same time as our Dad, we do know he was back at Stalag XXA by 10 December as Alistair writes:

'Left Külmsee 10th Dec for 13A. Still a miserable dump. Saw Allan & Archie – looking very fit. Lots of the boys there.'[1]

Alistair was only at Thorn for a few days however before joining a new work party headed for Godowicz.

During the latter half of 1941 a new barracks complex, called

Kopernicus (or Stalag 312 XXC), was built by British POWs under German direction. This was the camp that Alan had told us he eventually moved to sometime after October 1943. Situated near to the village of Glinki, to the south of Toruń, its main purpose was to accommodate the increasing number of Russian POWs.[2] Kopernicus was surrounded by barbed wire fences and made up of wooden huts, half of which housed Russian POWs while the other half of the camp held British POWs.

The Soviet Union had not signed the *Geneva Convention* and as a result the Germans treated the Russian POWs imprisoned here very badly. Propaganda led Germans to believe that most East Europeans, primarily Russians, Jews, Roma and Sinti were inferior, describing them as untermensch (sub-human).[3] The unfortunate Russian prisoners were used as slave labour, treated appallingly and thousands starved to death in indescribable conditions. Alan Moore told us that some Russian POW's were so hungry they resorted to cannibalism. He was occasionally able to pass food through the fence to the desperate men and heard from them that they knew they were going to die. They would either starve to death in the camp or be shot as deserters at the end of the war.

The former Glinki camp is now an empty space but the memorial board placed at the site states that from August 1941 until January 1945 over 21,000 Russians were imprisoned in Glinki. Approximately 14,000 died there and were buried in a mass grave in the forest close by.

In August when Dad arrived back at Stalag XXA it was likely that he was accommodated in one of the wooden barrack huts close to the forts. We think it was around this time that he heard about the conditions which the Russian prisoners had to endure and which he had spoken about in his later years.

Evidently the Allied POWs had been warned not to go near a wooden fence which separated the British and Russian prisoners at that time. However, when the guards were not watching Dad told us that one of the British inmates looked through a 'knothole' in the fence. He saw starving Russian POWs being forced to walk around a compound repeatedly, being beaten by the guards if they stumbled or fell. Dad also told us that the Russian prisoners were so desperately hungry they pulled tar from the roof to eat. These memories clearly haunted him. We later heard accounts which explained that on work parties the Russian POW's were always marched behind the British who would drop their cigarette ends for them to pick up.

January 1942

The start of a new year prompted Dad to start writing once more after a gap of six months. As yet another year in captivity began, it soon became clear that he was feeling very despondent. Despite being at such a low ebb he nevertheless managed to make diary entries for each month of 1942.

Thursday 1st January 1942
New Year's Day in writing only I'm afraid - holiday in the camp -no entertainment today unfortunately - everybody at a loose end - I am damned well fed up with everything - if not shifted will definitely go on transport soon.

Friday 2nd January 1942
No holiday today – still despondent – lots of snow these days – volunteered as sanitäter [medic or first-aider] on farm transport today but had no luck – attended pantomime at Fort XIII tonight which was quite enjoyable – had letter from Mother today & pleased to hear that my cards to her appear cheery!!!

On some empty pages at the back of the diary Dad wrote more detailed notes about how he was feeling on this date.

For lack of better material to fill these vacant pages I shall, when the spirit moves me, pen such thoughts, ideas, recurrences or impressions which may occur, be the mood black, white or the all too familiar grey. May any chance an unauthorised reader scan these pennings let him now at this early stage take heed of any frequent black moods, occasionally grey and almost extinct white – or is that all wrong??? Let him decide! Since the advent of the New Year, I feel that a subtle change has taken place. Can I possibly describe it in words or writing? I seem to remember such a – is it sensation – at some period before this damned war started. I am assuredly not myself. For an excellent reason, which I shall refrain from writing for many reasons, I am inexplicably disappointed and vexed. Is my choosing then so horribly incompetent and misleading to myself? An answer should be forthcoming in the near future if my surmise is correct! Two days later I am still in a grievous state of perplexity. I shall give it another couple of days.

Two more days have slipped by – or was it 22, I don't know!!! I believe the perplexity has eased considerably although not wholly or maybe I am just recovering from a very serious attack of fed up-ness. We assuredly have our bright moments – it more or less depends on the individual concerned. There are times when it must 'get you down'. After a considerable lapse I can now confidently write that I have got rid of the bogey, such as it was. The depression over …. [illegible words] has lifted! What! I should be a first class dart thrower by the time I leave this joint. Anything to keep the old mind occupied!!

For the first few weeks his mood remains very low.

Saturday 3rd January 1942
Just another day in this life or was it!!! Why did I? Snow still on the ground. Not so cold now. Bloody awful these days! What the hell is wrong??

Sunday 4th January 1942
Yesterday the pantomime commenced – the fort show was…. - I will bloody well go crackers in this joint – I will not be much longer in this place.

Monday 5th January 1942
Back to the old, old routine again – everybody is really browned off now – nothing of interest can take place now

Tuesday 6th January 1942
Just another day in this bloody life – I wonder how much longer this is going on

Wednesday 7th January 1942
.. I repeat the same old story – two sanitätors went to Thorn today. Archie unfortunately is unpaid – rumours of a further batch going down – sincerely hope we are lucky and remain together after so long.

Thursday 8th January 1942
Same old humdrum – Red X issue today – it barely relieves the monotony now

Friday 9th January 1942
Merely a repetition of the old story – rumour of more sanitätors going down to Thorn

Our father mentioned the possibility of going to work in Thorn on several occasions. This refers to the German hospital (Lazarette) in the town of Thorn where occasionally British RAMC personnel were employed. It was preferable to be working rather than moping around the camp as the days were long and tedious. Boredom was acute. Dad did not seem to be involved in any work details at this time, despite volunteering for jobs.

Saturday 10th January 1942
Merely a repetition of the old story once more – mail is slow these days – temperature about 10 degrees below – not too cold

Sunday 11th January 1942
Holiday if this word means anything now in this monotone called life – pantomime still running

Monday 12th January 1942
Still very cold in this place – fortunately we are not much outdoors

Tuesday 13th January 1942
Ditto – about 20 degrees below today – wrote letter home

The days passed very slowly at this time:

Not much to say these days – this month seems to pass very slowly

One more week has slipped by

Two more days has slipped by - or was it 22, I don't know!

Tensons sometimes built up among the men which was only to be expected when they were cooped up together in crowded accommodation day after day.

Sunday 18th January 1942
…Archie & I fell out with Ian today

Just four days after the falling out however, Ian, Archie and Dad were once more back on good terms.

This quote from *The Barbed Wire University* illustrates that disagreements were not uncommon.

'Tempers are getting somewhat 'edgy' now. I suppose this is inevitable and really it is surprising that things are not much worse than they really are. However, every now and then we get a flare up, usually over nothing at all and a most personal argument, coupled with really foul language takes place, no-one has gone for the throat yet.' [4]

Yet, despite the occasional squabbles, most of the time they all made efforts to get along and help one another in any way they could.

A Moore kindly gave me a towel today

Monday 19th January 1942
Still frosty – not much snow so far – Red Cross has become very scarce – 'one does not miss the water till the well runs dry'

Tuesday 20th January 1942
Cold & frosty – usually about 20 degrees below these days

Wednesday 21st January 1942
Ditto. Issue of much needed Red Cross today – it is slow in coming thru these days

Thursday 22nd January 1942
Spring cleaning the old bed today – reunited with Ian at his own request – had Xmas card from Jean – working with Alan Moore from today – 7 sanitätors went to Thorn

For most of January the weather remained bitterly cold, Red Cross parcels were scarce, mail was less frequent - all in all not a good time. Dad says that he was now working with Alan Moore, so we know Dad, Archie and Alan were again together.

Friday 23rd January 1942
Still cold – snowed a little today – excellent reports from RAMC boys at Thorn

Saturday 24th January 1942
Still cold but bearable – concert tonight – but did not attend – showing again tomorrow

Sunday 25th January 1942
Coldest day this winter – but only 28 degrees below – attended concert for a short time. Wrote PC home and one to Canada.

Tuesday 27th January 1942
Cold – issue of Canadian parcel & 50 cigs today – went down with stretcher party to Fort 14 - had two tins of milk from Harry Morris

Wednesday 28th January 1942
Still frosty – no baths this week due to breakdown

Thursday 29th January 1942
Not so cold today – thawing slightly – had no mail now since quite a time

Dad wrote further notes in the back of his diary.

Today is 29th January. It has been a slow month in passing. I must confess to myself that I have been pretty fed up since the advent of the New Year. I think the trouble is the necessity of a change from this place. I don't think it can come quick enough

30th January 1942
Only one more day of this month left as I write. Disturbing news these days of German success in Africa. Hitler is giving a speech tonight. I wonder if there will be anything of importance disclosed? Incidentally, I am writing this in bed as we have the luxury of a bed light. For how long, I wonder??!

Having been at Thorn for over six months now, Dad was increasingly desperate for a change and was still feeling low as February came around

Friday 6th February 1942
Still cold – letter from Mother today – gambling tonight again & had a little luck

Saturday 7th February 1942
..... Maillie [?] was unfortunate in burning his kit bag this morning – Dodd's bed went on fire tonight

On 8 February it is noted in the diary that they had photographs taken in the camp:

Photographs taken in camp today - was included in 3 large groups and one small one (five of us) - taken by civvies.

Dad had a number of photographs taken whilst he was a POW including the one shown overleaf which we believe may be a copy of one taken on 8 February. These posed photographs were possibly used by the German army for propaganda purposes showing the men apparently fit and well.

The majority of our father's photographs appear to be official POW group photos with the name of the camp stamped on the back. Some have his room number and name pencilled on but there are no dates or names recorded. Visual clues like the level of snow in the photo and the amount of clothing worn can help to indicate rough dates and our father with his black wavy hair and taller-than-average height is easy to recognise in the group shots. Dad sent a small group photograph home to Inverness as a postcard, dated April 1942.

Other photos in his collection were those sent to him by family and friends including some of the Taj Mahal from a Canadian acquaintance. Most, however, are family snaps sent from home by our grandmother with the message 'Best love...' or 'Warmest love... from Mum' and dates written carefully on the back.

All incoming and outgoing mail was heavily censored by the German authorities. Letters sent to the POWs were not permitted to contain any information about the armed forces, the war effort, politics, food or rations. They had to be no longer than two sides of notepaper, otherwise delivery would be delayed or even stopped.[5] Dad received a number of photographs from home, but these may have been included in a parcel rather than a letter.

Diaries kept by POWs were also subject to censorship and confiscation during the frequent unannounced searches which could take place at any time.

> 'If taken away but deemed safe and innocuous by their captors, the diary ..... would be stamped by the camp censors and returned to its author. If the contents .... revealed behaviour that broke the rules, these narratives could be confiscated or the author severely punished.'[6]

Most POWs therefore self-censored their diary entries and made

15. POWs at Stalag XXA. Dad is second from right.

16. Outside accommodation hut 3A at Stalag XXA. Dad is third from left and Archie Dey is on far left, both in back row. Standing next to Dad on far right is another RAMC member, Private Samuel Bowden.

no mention of conditions in the camp. The reality of life in captivity for the ordinary soldier remained for the most part unrecorded at the time. Many men were told to destroy any diaries they had kept before returning home, so we were fortunate that our father's diaries survived. After the war, however, some ex-POWs, like Alistair MacRitchie, wrote fuller accounts of their wartime experiences from memory. Dad's diaries, however, were purely notes he had made at the time with no evidence he had added to them after his return to the UK.

> *February is now a week old. It is still fairly cold off and on. I guess I am pretty near the end of my tether in this dump – been over six months here. Should know by the end of this month when I am likely to move, of course I may be shifted quicker than I expect! I am hoping to see something big and unexpected happening this spring. I wonder if J is really doing well in Africa. He is definitely not keeping us alive!*

> **Wednesday 11th February 1942**
> *Another week has started but more days or weeks do not mean anything here. Is the aforementioned so and so beginning to prevail again? I hope not. The prop is rather pessimistic these days but it's not taken too seriously in these quarters. Incidentally, naval commissions seem fashionable at home e.g., John Main, Brian Shaw etc.*

> **Monday 16th February 1942**
> *Yet another week – it does not seem of much avail writing the same damned thing in each – had letter from home – A Moore working in dispensary in Stalag – saw Taylor today about Thorn*

Alan Moore worked in Fort XIV (the camp hospital) and Dad still saw him occasionally when, for instance, he was called up for stretcher duty at the hospital:

> *Today is the 18th February but it does not mean a thing. The chief item of interest these days is the position of Singapore. I think we are still safe there yet and likely to be*

for some time. It appears from the weather these days that an early Spring is likely. The last few days have been quite sunny altho' there is still quite a lot of snow on the ground. Quite a change from last winter when balaclavas were the order of the day. I may not be feeling it so bad since I am not out so much, a walk round the fort is very invigorating these days. It is about the only exercise we can get in this dump!! I do not think a spot of arbeit [work] would do any harm if it would only hurry up and come. I must repeat my previous statement that I am about the end of my tether!!!

Although boredom remained a huge problem, sometimes a simple thing like a beautiful bright and sunny day could lift the mood for a short while. Dad wrote some extended notes for the first spring-like day:

Sunday 22nd February 1942

Not so cold – really a glorious morning – spent morning walking round top of Fort 13 – sledging up there

Today is Sunday 22nd February. Really a spring morning – glorious sunshine & just that nip in the air. It was good to hear the Red X rep took such an interest in questions put forward. We hope that investigations will terminate in ultimate success or at least satisfaction – not so bad these days!!

In addition to sledging that Dad mentions, Alan Moore also told us that the POWs (including Dad, Alan and Archie), sometimes played ice hockey on the frozen moat. They were able to obtain a pair of ice skates which they initially took turns in using. When they eventually received more skates via the Red Cross, they were able to play improvised games of ice hockey using sticks. Although sports clothing and even repair kits were sometimes provided in the parcels, they still often had to make do with what they could fashion for themselves. An ice hockey puck was made from a Cherry Blossom boot polish tin with the lid nailed down and a wooden block fitted inside to give it weight. According to Alan Moore they first had to ask permission from the guards to go out on the frozen moat otherwise they would fire shots above their heads and order them back in. However, when games were actually in progress the guards sometimes came over to watch! The POWs became experts at finding ingenious ways to occupy themselves with the little available to them.

Alan also remembered that on occasion, during the summer months, the German guards would bring their wives or girlfriends along to go boating on the moats.

News from the outside world was still reaching the men, perhaps with the help of Alan's radio, as in the early part of February Dad twice mentions the grave situation in Singapore. The fall of Singapore to the Japanese was one of the greatest of Britain's defeats during the war and although our father's comments are brief and give nothing away, news like this must have been a heavy blow for the men desperately hoping for an Allied victory so that the war would come to an end and they could all go home.

Towards the end of February Dad was given a chance to start work in the camp laundry:

Wednesday 25th February 1942
Still thawing – got word tonight to start in laundry tomorrow – (ten new men) – it is hellish to be short of a smoke

Thursday 26th February 1942
Colder today – started work at 7.30am – rather different to what I expected – finished at 4.30pm – we must get a smoke

Friday 27th February 1942
Cold again this morning - put in second days work – Miller takes my place tomorrow- Mackillop on job today – had letter from Mother tonight (5th Jan) – parcel between 4 & 12 cig each today.

He only lasted a couple of days at the laundry and was not impressed by either the conditions or the type of work he had to do…

I never at any time had any inclination to sample the famous laundry, far less work permanently there. I feel

*now after two days experience that my instinct has been
fully justified. To spend approximately 7 hours each day
in such an atmosphere for one thing is contrary to my idea
of a fairly healthy job. A breath of real fresh air after that
lot just about knocks me dizzy. I consider it very doubtful
as a sanitätors job! The advantages seem to be at a minus.
Or are the women? such a great attraction?? Maybe some
blokes are more easily pleased than others.*

There was also a shortage of cigarettes in the camp around this
time. Many of the men had become heavy smokers so it became a
problem when supplies were scarce.

Friday 13th March 1942
Cold, it is hellish to have no smokes

Sunday 15th March 1942
*Mild today – quiet as usual – wrote letter card to Mother
– deloused today. Archie & I spraying the beds with Jeyes.*

Monday 16th March 1942
*Mild today – Red X bulk issue of chocs, jams, sugar, soap,
cigs, cheese & milk – down at Fort 14 with stretcher party
today – no light in hut tonight*

Tuesday 17th March
*Quite mild today – the ground is very muddy – had 2
letters from Mother, one from Milly & one from Canada
– Archie up at fort tonight seeing Taffy – carbide lamps in
hut tonight*

Friday 20th March 1942
*Very cold indeed today, that wind bites into one's bones –
got white loaf. Archie gave Scottie scarf for tobacco – smokes
are damned scarce again*

The prisoners were also allowed to receive theatrical accessories
and before long they were putting on shows and stage plays like *The
Case of the Frightened Lady* which was produced by the men in the

'Camp 13A Repertory Company'. Occasional evenings of mainly home-grown entertainment helped to break up the daily tedium.

Fancy dress dance tonight – not too bad

Warm – attended band show in the evening – it was first class

Saw play 'The Case of the Frightened Lady' tonight – quite good

In amongst Dad's memorabilia there are also photographs which illustrated other aspects of camp life. Some show men dressed for their parts in plays they put on, complete with handmade backdrops and props to make their productions as convincing as possible. Others show the band members with their instruments.

But, in general, March 1942 was marked by boredom, a shortage of cigarettes and food, slow mail, a spell of very cold weather and a lack of Red Cross parcels. Dad did not seem to be assigned to a labour party during this time but was working for spells at Fort XIV on stretcher duty and at the laundry. The weather did start to improve during the last few days of the month however and he was even able to exchange his wooden clogs for boots again at Stalag XXA.

Tuesday 24th March 1942
Warmer – warm and spring like – it is about five weeks since we had a Red Cross parcel – wrote PC to Mother & one to Canada; exchanged clogs for boots at Stalag

However, only a week or so later an entry states;

'flogged boots for meat & bread'

Wednesday 8th April 1942
issue of 50 cigs today – what a Godsend – heard of job in library

Thursday 9th April 1942
Very warm & pleasant these days – started work in library today – Alan Moore went to Fort 14

Fort XIV was the camp hospital and Alan later told us that he eventually ended up in charge of the hospital kitchen there.

With the arrival of equipment for indoor games from the Red Cross, Dad became involved in playing table tennis. This was probably where he picked up his fondness and considerable skills for the game.

On April 27 Dad received a blow when Archie, his companion for the past two and a half years, was detailed for transport and was due to leave early the following morning. There was nothing either of them could do of course and he felt the loss of his friend keenly:

Miss Archie today - the camp is very empty now

Sunday 3rd May 1942
Warmer, attended Band & Crooning Competition (13A won both) served cocoa and sandwiches afterwards – saw Cpl Ross – shifted from Stalag Hut to Black Hut

The Black Huts, so called because of their colour, were used for accommodation like the main Stalag huts and contained three-tier bunk beds with straw mattresses. Alistair also mentions that they were used to accommodate 'floating personnel'.

The weather continued to improve throughout May. Having spent about twenty days in the Black Hut Dad was then returned to the Stalag Huts. There is no mention of work at this time, but he does say he was getting good at table tennis!

After a long gap with no deliveries there was also a welcome issue of a Red Cross parcel each;

Saturday 9th May 1942
Warm today – very pleasant surprise today – had issue of Red X parcel each – first since February – Scottie on transport

In May of 1942 the British Red Cross started production of a free monthly magazine for the relatives of the POWs called *The Prisoner of War* and was the official journal of the Prisoners of War Department of the Red Cross and St. John War Organisation. Its purpose was to give those at home an idea of the conditions in the camps and how the men spent their time as POWs. It published articles on what to include in parcels, stories from the prisoners in the camps themselves and even photos of the men engaged in drama productions, boxing matches and so on. After the war many believed it gave a very sanitised version of the POW experience and was perhaps designed to reassure families that their men were 'doing OK' and did not give an entirely accurate reflection of camp life. Our grandmother received this magazine and indeed, several copies survived and were found in Dad's suitcase.

The ICRC also carried out visits to the POW camps to check that the men were being treated in accordance with the Geneva Convention and they would report news of these visits in the magazine. In the 18 May 1942 edition, there is a snippet about a visit to Stalag XXA which says:

> 'The British dentist at XIIIA is allowed to operate in all the principal work camps. Fort XIV – at this time of year patients are able to be out in the sun all day, on the moat and in the gardens.' [7]

ICRC visits were planned in advance and although there may have been occasions when hasty improvements were made ahead of the visit, the ICRC delegate was usually able to ask the camp leader privately if this was the case. He would meet with the camp leader, the medical officer and the chaplain who would often have reports to submit and lists of POWs with no news from home. The delegate would have the opportunity to talk to the prisoners and ask about their general conditions and POWs could arrange to speak privately if they wished. He was often the only direct link between the inmates and the outside world and sometimes brought relief supplies with him or made arrangements for the arrival of food, clothing, games, books and medicines etc.[8]

Monday 18th May 1942
Very warm – had note from Archie – he seems to be going on OK – won my game in Table Tennis League

At last, on the first of June 1942 some work came Dad's way –

Rude awakening at 5am. Detailed to leave at 7 o'clock - to Posen we thought: landed at Thorn Lazarette - started work almost right away - plenty of work & dirty work for Jerry patients

The Lazarette was the German hospital in the town of Thorn which we believe housed some of the more seriously ill British POWs as well as German patients. By day three however, Dad had handed his name in to get back to the Stalag:

Tuesday 2nd June 1942
Long day from 7 till 9.30 – too much

The remainder of June and then July come and go with little of note in Dad's diaries – many letters were written, and he works for a spell in the Rec Room. We know he did some studying for accountancy exams whilst a POW and he writes on 10 September;

Received accounting books from library!

POWs were encouraged to engage not only in sporting activities but also to read and study whilst in captivity as stated in *The Convention relative to the treatment of prisoners of war – Geneva 27 July 1929*, Article 17: 'belligerents shall encourage as much as possible the organisation of intellectual and sporting pursuits by the prisoners of war.'[9]

During 1940, the ICRC were able to obtain permission for British POWs to follow correspondence courses using material published by technical colleges and universities in the United Kingdom.[10] The Educational Books Section of the British Red Cross POW Department made arrangements for 'blue forms' to be sent to the camps which the POWs could use to request books to assist with their studies.[11] For example, Dad wrote a list of topics studied including 'Criminal Law, Wills & Trusts, Mercantile Law and Rights & Duties of Liquidators, Trustees & Receivers'

The Prisoner of War, the official journal of the Prisoners of War Department of the Red Cross and St. John War Organisation, included the following article in March 1943:

> 'Serious Study in Camp
>
> The quality of the results now coming through indicates that a good deal of serious study is being carried on in these camps," writes the External Registrar of London University, who kindly undertakes the work of issuing and collecting examination papers for prisoners of war on behalf of the Red Cross Educational Books section. Thanks to the helpful co-operation of the Postal and Censorship authorities, delays in transit both ways have been reduced to a minimum.' [12]

However, physical activities were still important for Dad and he also speaks about playing in football leagues against the other forts;

> *played football against Fort XI – got beat 6-1 (I scored)*

There are very few entries for the month of September but in early October Dad is detailed for work at Fort 15 which seems to suit him.

Monday 5th October 1942
30 sanitätors detailed for Fort 15 today – I among them... arrived here about 5pm – seems good!!

Tuesday 6th October 1942
Roll 9am instead of 6.30 – pleasant change – rackets etc seem OK!

Although the daily routine varied from one camp to another, one constant feature was the parade for roll call which would take place at least once each day.

Dad doesn't speak about the type of work he does at Fort 15, but other activities seem to be keeping him occupied!

> *went to dancing lesson - think I'll do OK*

and

> *...took part in sports today*

attended second dancing lesson

went to dancing tonight – Harry is a big help

We confess to being curious about the dancing lessons…

His twenty-fourth birthday on 18 October passed without incident and is mentioned almost as an aside;

24 today - got 5 cigs from J first thing this morning - wrote letter to Mother, Milly, PC to Jess & one to Canada

Throughout this time his mother continued to write numerous letters and Dad never failed to mention what mail he received. An extra note too brought welcome news;

Got note from Mac along with parcel of sugar - Archie is OK

[Mac was shorthand for Alistair MacRitchie who was away from Stalag XXA on work parties at this time.]

A couple of days after this Dad writes a postcard to Mrs Dey (Archie's mother) - perhaps to pass on the news that Archie was well.

Wrote PC to Mother & one to Mrs Dey

November has very few entries save to mention that he reached the semi-final in the quoits match and then went on to win the competition the following week:

Won quoits final. Got trophy & 300 Marks!!!

Dad brought home a rope quoit with a plaque attached which we assume was his winning 'trophy'.

Although the men found activities to keep them occupied as best they could, in reality the days could be long and tedious, especially when they were not out on work parties.

Towards the end of December 1942 Dad received three book parcels for his correspondence course and had a nice surprise when unexpectedly on the twenty-third, Archie arrived back at Stalag XXA.

17. Rope quoit won by Dad whilst at Stalag XXA.

Wednesday 23rd December 1942
Very pleasant surprise today – Archie arrived with a big party from Fort 13 – unluckily he is due for transport again. Saw Granger and also Col Mackay

Col Mackay was the Commanding Officer of 153 FA.

On Christmas Day in 1940 food was rationed, no entertainment was permitted and everyone was made to work as punishment for some POWs slipping past the guards to bring food back into the camp. Things were very different in 1942. They were served a 'first class dinner' and enjoyed an evening concert with drinks:

Friday 25th December 1942
Xmas day – enjoyable day – first class dinner – roast veal, beef, gravy, pots, pea soup etc – concert and drinks at night – returned about 3am

Saturday 26th December 1942
More Xmas celebrations – weather fairly good – no word of Archie's party going yet. Hoping he will be here at least over New Year

Thursday 31st December 1942
Remember Port & Polish wine! Had 5 letters this week

Although Archie's name was up for transport again just the day after he got back to camp, it turned out he did not leave until February. Archie and Dad had a few weeks to enjoy one another's company again.

There are diary entries for just the first three months of 1943, mainly about letters written and received.

Sunday 10th January 1943
Letter to Mother and one to Willie. PC to Milly and one to Phyllis

Friday 29th January 1943
Had letter from Mother – first this year

Saturday 6th February 1943
Received October clothing parcel

Finally, the day came when his friend Archie was due for transport:

Friday 12th February 1943
Archie went on transport to Strasburg – could not get off

Strasburg was a town near Toruń, now known as Brodnica.

There was also a brief reunion with another of his good friends, Alistair:

Sunday 28th February 1943
Mac came back here last week. Wrote PC to the camp for unclaimed parcel. PC to Mother

Amongst our father's photographs were several taken at an athletic event. A team picture shows Dad dressed in a singlet with the Union

18. British Athletics Team at Stalag XXA. Dad is pictured seated centre, second row from front.

19. POW band, Stalag XXA.

flag and the year '1943' sewn on to the front. In another photograph an Australian athletics team poses for the camera. They were members of the 2/5 Australian General Hospital (AGH) captured in Greece in 1941 who were also POWs at Fort XV.

Dad's final diary entry was made on Sunday 21st March 1943:

> *Letter to Mother, letter to Canada, PC to Sir J Lorne McLeod.*

Sir John Lorne MacLeod was a prominent Edinburgh solicitor who served on Edinburgh City Council and was also Lord Provost and Lord Lieutenant of Edinburgh. He held a number of other positions including Chairman of the General Nursing Council for Scotland and Chairman of the Scottish Life Assurance Company. [13] Although Dad does not say why he wrote to him, he may have been enquiring about options to resume his law studies.

As we turned over the last page of his diary, we paused to reflect on the momentous events that had unfolded. As a young man celebrating his twenty-first birthday in Inverness in 1939 Dad could never have imagined how much his life would change in the space of just one year. He would go from being on active duty in France as a Nursing Orderly, treating the terrible injuries of the war-wounded whilst coming under attack, to being captured by the enemy and used as forced labour at a prison camp far from home.

At the time of writing his final diary entry he had been away from home for almost three and a half years, but this was not the end of his story. We now had to look elsewhere to find out what happened to him next.

Eleven

Connections

December 2012 to April 2014

Just weeks after our meeting with Alan and Hilda in Selkirk a Christmas card arrived through the post from Yorkshire with a 'news alert.' Our group photograph was going to be shown on the Antiques Roadshow!

When the BBC discovered that Alan had met up with us as a result of his appearance on the Remembrance Special programme, a photo of this meeting, alongside Alan's original interview, was scheduled to be broadcast on their forthcoming Antiques Roadshow Christmas Special. The show was aired on 23 December 2012 and Alan's story was described as one of their most moving wartime accounts.

As Alan was keen to find others who had known him from Stalag XXA, we all agreed that it was a good time to bring his story to the attention of our local press. As the Highlands had been the heartland of the 51st Division it was possible that POW veterans or their close relatives may still live in the area. The story was also of local interest as Dad had been brought up in Inverness and had lived in Nairn since the early 1960s. Alistair also had strong Highland connections as he had spent his early years in Fort William.

In January 2013 the *Inverness Courier* and the *Nairnshire Telegraph* published an account of how we had all met up in Selkirk along with an invitation for any surviving veterans to contact us on Alan's behalf. Although we did not hear from any former members of the 51st, we were contacted by relatives whose fathers or uncles had been POWs in Poland and heard fascinating stories and anecdotes from the war which had survived.

We heard of one British prisoner who had sabotaged engine repairs deliberately to frustrate the German war effort. Another POW took the blame for trying to smuggle a tool past the guards after returning with a work party and on this occasion his quick action thankfully saved a Polish Jew from severe punishment.

Some weeks later we received a welcome phone call from a Peter McLoughlin, who was a regular volunteer at the Regimental Museum of the Highlanders (Seaforth and Camerons). This museum is located in Fort George on the coast of the Moray Firth, only twelve miles east of Inverness. Built in 1746, the fort today still serves as an army barracks. From our father's service records we also knew that Fort George was a place well known to him.

Peter was interested in our story as his late uncle had also spent years of captivity as a POW in Poland. But as Peter had just recently organised a trip to visit Stalag XXA in Toruń, it was agreed that we should meet up with him on his return.

By July 2013 we had finished transcribing Dad's diaries and had more time to spend on background research. We were interested in finding out more about the RAMC and had contacted the Museum of Military Medicine in Aldershot for information. Although specific details could not be released, the staff were extremely helpful and were able to give us an informative insight into the basic training that was in place for Field Ambulance personnel in 1939.

Although it was Crookham where Dad had trained, it was Woolmanhill Barracks in Aberdeen that had been the 153 FA depot between 1938 and 1947. Aberdeen was also home to the Gordon Highlanders infantry regiment which had been part of the BEF in 1940. Today Aberdeen is the location of the well-respected Gordon

Highlanders Museum that opened to the public in 1997. It had come highly recommended by Alan and Hilda as they had previously made a visit and been impressed by the staff's willingness and enthusiasm in helping Alan to try and contact men who had once served in the 153 FA. Many descendants of WW2 veterans came forward but unfortunately no former members from the field ambulance unit could be traced. When we visited the Gordon Highlanders Museum ourselves in 2013, we discovered the staff had made contact with a veteran from the 153 FA and we were able to pass details on to Alan.

Later in the summer we caught up again with Hilda and Alan in Yorkshire. It was a pleasure to join them on a drive through the North Yorkshire Dales and to see the nearby Catterick Garrison. When the conversation turned to the past, we heard more fascinating stories about Alan's wartime experiences and Hilda and Alan's recent trip to Stalag XXA. While in Toruń they also visited Glinki to see the former site of the camp (Kopernicus) where Alan had spent his final months in captivity. They also paid their respects at the nearby Russian POW mass burial site.

Although we still hoped that our frequent internet searches might throw up information which would lead us to Archie Dey nothing ever came to light. Luckily, we did manage to uncover more about Dad's Glasgow wartime friend Johnnie McComiskey after contacting his son Angus through the internet. When Angus and his elder brother Jim were growing up in Glasgow, they remembered meeting many of their father's post-war pals including our Dad, known to them as 'Uncle Allan'. Like us, they had recollections of visits from our family during the late 1950s and early 1960s as well as memories of a visit they made to Nairn in 1966. From the collective information that we now had, it seemed likely that Johnnie had not been a POW at Stalag XXA but had spent the war years in Stalag XXB in Marienburg.

A few weeks later we heard from Peter at Fort George and a meeting to learn about his trip to Poland was arranged. While in Toruń Peter had been shown around Stalag XXA by Piotr, a local historian and guide who had recently featured on a BBC Alba television documentary called From Stalag to Gulag.

Not only was Piotr a local resident of Toruń, he was also an avid and enthusiastic collector of war artefacts and in his spare time had created a small museum. After showing Peter our father's assortment of memorabilia he was sure that Piotr would be extremely interested to see them and gave us his contact details. We emailed Piotr and arranged to send pictures of Dad's wartime ephemera and copies of his photos from Stalag XXA. This was to be the start of many months of correspondence as we exchanged information.

At the beginning of November Peter contacted us again as he was organising a presentation about Stalag XXA at the Highlanders Museum and asked if we would like to participate. Peter talked about his recent visit to Toruń while Dad's diaries and memorabilia illustrated what life had been like for British POWs. The evening, presented by Fiona and Peter, was a success and well attended.

The idea of us making a visit to Toruń in the near future was now becoming more of a possibility. Piotr, who was keen to thank us for sending material for his museum, had now offered to be our guide when we visited. There were no 'ifs' or 'buts!'

Historic Toruń

We made plans to visit Toruń in April 2014. But a month before we were due to leave for Poland a headline in *The Guardian* on 1st March read,

> 'Russian "invasion" of Crimea fuels fear of Ukraine conflict'[1]

There was a sense of nervousness in the region. It seemed ironic that there was talk of aggression as we were preparing to find out more about a war that began over seventy years ago.

As we began to make definite travel plans family interest in our trip had grown and by the time we left Scotland we had reached the grand total of seven! Fiona had been joined by her partner Iain, and Lauren their daughter. I would be travelling with my husband Eddie and our

149

son and daughter, Allan and Laura. Each family travelled to Poland by different routes, but we arranged to meet up in Toruń town centre on Tuesday 8 April 2014.

Fiona and her family first visited the city of Poznań or 'Posen' as Dad had noted in a diary entry. It was a town that had also been no stranger to the atrocities of war. In October 1939 Fort VII also known as Konzentrationslager Posen was the first concentration camp set up in occupied Poland. It was also where early experiments on execution by gas chamber were carried out.[2] Exact numbers of those who died here and in the surrounding forest are estimated to be in the thousands.[3]

After Toruń, Fiona and her family planned a visit to Gdansk (formerly Danzig) and the nearby Stutthof concentration camp. Stutthof was a Nazi concentration camp for Jews and political prisoners and as many as 65,00 people died here. During the war years, both Graudenz and Stalag XXA were sub-camps of Stutthof. Nowadays the site has been preserved as a museum and is open to the public to visit.

Meanwhile, we flew to Warsaw where eighty-five per cent of the city had been destroyed during the war. Here we met the historian and author Peter Pininski, who in his books *The Stuarts Last Secret* and *Bonnie Prince Charlie – A Life*, documents his descent from the royal Stuarts. Peter took us on an historical walking tour of Warsaw's Old Town which had been rebuilt after the war and also generously gave his time to source background information about wartime Toruń.

When we all met up in Toruń as arranged, our first impression was of a delightful, picturesque city steeped in history. Red slate-roofed buildings and cobbled streets blended with busy open-air restaurants, bars and shops. We just had time to brush up on our guidebook Polish before checking into our accommodation. Both apartments ('Apartamenty Toruń') were located in the vicinity of the Grand Square. Although modernised inside, the apartments were housed in traditional sixteenth-century buildings situated in the heart of the Old Town.

Finding Piotr's address was our first priority and when we asked for directions at the tourist office, we were surprised to find that they knew him well – it seemed that our guide was both well-known and influential and had 'keys to many doors.' It was a promising start.

Our meeting place was the local high school where Piotr worked as a German language teacher and it was in the basement of this school where his Historical Museum (Muzeum Historyczno-Wojskowe) was located. We were warmly greeted and Piotr wasted no time in making us feel welcome.

Concrete steps took us down to the museum. The treasure trove of World War Two exhibits ranged from a sentry box to an army uniform button and Piotr's knowledge and enthusiasm for this period of Toruń's history was obvious. A glass cabinet containing well-preserved documents and blocks of soap reputedly from Stutthof prison camp left us wondering if this might have been the latherless soap that Dad had often spoken about.

One corner of the room was dedicated to items connected to the Allied POWs. Barbed wire, uniform remnants, a 51st Highland Division emblem, a tin of hair cream and pieces of Red Cross food containers had been salvaged and displayed. A kilted mannequin of a Scottish soldier gifted by the Highlanders Museum at Fort George stood nearby.

Photographs that we had sent to Piotr, showing groups of POWs featuring British and Australian sports teams, were on display. We were delighted to see that some prints had also been used to make a video presentation alongside re-enactment scenes which had been filmed at the forts by senior school students.

In one small area, part of a hospital ward had been replicated. The furniture displayed indicated that this would have been the layout used for the treatment of officers in Fort XIV. Other patients would not have had the luxury of wardrobe space to hang their clothes. A box of basic medical equipment lay nearby.

As we left the museum, we paused at a table to sign the visitors book. The wooden desk appeared unremarkable until we learned that

20. Interior of museum showing typical POW bunk bed. Reproduced by kind permission of Piotr Olecki.

21. Museum interior showing some of the items on display

during the war it had been used as a POW registration table in Stalag XXA. As we touched the well-worn surface we wondered if this might have been the very desk which Dad and Alan had once stood beside in July 1940. Our visit had given us a fascinating insight into the history of Stalag XXA and Toruń during the war years and the museum's existence in a town where people may understandably wish to forget the past, is an achievement. Many more exhibits are still kept in storage as the search for larger premises continues. But now it was time for a brisk walking tour of the Old Town with Piotr.

Toruń, in the Pomeranian region of Poland, is often referred to as Little Kraków or as 'Kraków of the north'. Historically it is a mix of German and Polish influences and its origins go back to 1231 when it was founded by the powerful and widespread military and religious Teutonic Order. The Teutonic Knights built a fortified base and castle in Toruń in their quest to spread Christianity throughout Eastern Europe. Eventually Toruń became a prominent trade centre and the largest and most important city in the region.

During World War Two Toruń was fortunate to be one of the few Polish cities that did not suffer considerable damage and we could see that its medieval brick Gothic architecture had been remarkably well preserved. Recent conservation projects have involved restoring buildings to their original colours. Toruń is also the birthplace of the astronomer Nicolaus Copernicus and a museum and monument pay honour to his scientific achievements.

With the help of Piotr's local knowledge of the medieval centre we saw the building which in the 1940s housed the Lazarette where Dad once worked. Although no longer a hospital the building is still in use. Piotr also pointed out the former premises of the town laundry where we believe Dad also briefly worked.

Not only had we learned about the past, but we had also discovered the delights of modern-day Toruń. It is a place which is now a World Heritage Site and believed by many to be one of the most beautiful medieval cities in Europe.

Toruń Fortress

It was Wednesday 9 April 2014. We had considered making the ninety-minute train journey to Grudziądz (formerly Graudenz) to see the town where Dad had been captive for a year. However, unlike Toruń, we were told that there is now little evidence of the war era left. The building once used to accommodate the British POWs has been demolished and no records of the German street names, known to

Dad in 1941, could be accessed. Having made the decision not to visit Grudziądz, we instead took the opportunity to visit the famous Toruń gingerbread factory, to bake some 'pierniki toruńskie' before meeting up with Piotr for our tour of Stalag XXA later in the day.

The city of Toruń is divided by the Vistula River, historically a vital trading route in Poland and part of the landscape of many important Polish cities. Yet, looking at the quiet, flowing water and peaceful surroundings there was no hint of the turmoil that it had witnessed over the years. On the opposite side of this legendary river were the forts that we had come to visit.

As our taxi crossed the Jósef Piłsudski bridge to the left bank of the Vistula River the landscape and atmosphere could not have been more different. The sky darkened and rain clouds gathered. Historical buildings were replaced by concrete block houses, small factories, storage buildings, garages and waste ground. Somewhere in amongst it all were a number of the forts once known collectively as Stalag XXA.

Out first stop was beyond Toruń's main train station where lay a long straight stretch of railway line. There were some discarded wagons and rough grass and gravel. This was the spot where, seventy-four years ago, thousands of POWs disembarked from crowded cattle trucks and where armed guards were lined up ready to march the men to the camp. Nearby was an ominous lookout tower to deter any prisoners from making a bid for freedom. 'No escape!' said Piotr.

Through the heavy rain our first sight of Stalag XXA was the now privately-owned Fort XV where Dad had been once been accommodated. However, the huge steel doors were firmly locked and the high stone walls and railings meant that only a glimpse of the fort was possible. Our next stop at Fort XIV was to be very different.

Approaching the former camp hospital, we could clearly see red brick walls through the iron fence and barbed wire. As the gates opened a low building came into view. A wide moat with grassy banks and trees curled around the fort. Today fish swim and breed undisturbed in the deep water. It was a peaceful scene and our thoughts drifted back to Alan's stories of rowing boats and games of

22. Fort XIV exterior view.

23. Fort XIV interior of ward.

155

ice hockey. Piled under a tree, remnants of rusty metal hospital beds reminded us of the fort's former use.

No value can be placed on that moment when the door to Fort XIV opened and we were able to step inside and walk along the very corridors which Dad would have known. We had walked straight into the past.

Wandering through arched whitewashed tunnels, touching cold brick walls and squinting through the dusty glass windows, we could imagine echoes of footsteps and voices of many nationalities mingling in the background. And somewhere down one of those corridors was the loose brick masking the cavity where Alan had secretly hidden his radio.

Painted numbers on the solid wooden doors leading to the wards were still legible, hospital furniture was stacked in rickety piles and a metal ladder leading to a lookout tower which Fiona ventured up was intact. We saw where the beds in the wards would have been placed and spaces where fires were once lit were visible, although it remained cool inside those subterranean fortresses, even in the summer. During the bitter winter, temperatures could drop dramatically and sometimes it became so cold that cups of drinking water would freeze. The visit to Fort XIV alone would have been more than worth the journey to Poland but there was still more to see.

A short drive took us to Fort XIII or the British Fort as it was once called. It was a place where Dad had attended concerts and plays and once wrote that he had spent the morning 'walking round top of Ft 13 - sledging up there.' A hutted area (XIIIA) was used as overflow accommodation and although the huts are long gone, we could still see where they once stood.

The fort itself is now occupied by the Polish military and we waited as a line of armoured vehicles carrying armed soldiers passed by. We also saw the white two-storey building which had been the camp headquarters from early 1940 and next to that the distribution centre for POW mail and parcels.

During the war some rooms in the headquarters building had

156

24. Reservoir near Fort XI where POWs sometimes bathed.

25. Entrance to Fort XI

157

beenused for printing and photography and we learned that it was here where the monthly *Prisoner's Pie* magazine compiled by POWs at Stalag XXA was published. In the early days it was printed every fortnight and featured camp news, stories and cartoons. A weekly paper called *The Camp* was also produced here and distributed to British POWs at the sub-camp in Grudziądz.

En route to Fort XI we took a short diversion to see the railway siding at Schlüsselmühle, now known as Toruń Kluczyki. During the war British POWs were involved in expanding facilities at this location. It was here where the offices of Siemens had been located.

Heading towards the entrance to Fort XI we passed a small reservoir that had been used as a swimming pool by the prisoners. We suspect that this was also where the new arrivals may have been stripped, washed and deloused as described by Alistair in his narrative. A flat area where a garage now stands had once been a football pitch and was where a prisoner had been shot for straying too close to the boundary. Near the fort was an area of rough ground where overflow hutted accommodation (XIA) had been built in 1940 and where Dad had once been accommodated. The fort itself was surrounded by thick vegetation and a deep dry grassy moat. It was in serious disrepair, but we had come here specifically to see something extraordinary which had been uniquely preserved.

Inside the fort a damp musty smell lingered in every crack as by torchlight we picked our way through dark corridors of rubble and down steps to where the washrooms and kitchens had once been. Sadly, vandalism had recently reduced the kitchen stove to a pile of bricks. Going deeper underground, we eventually reached a small room. It was here where those who had broken camp rules were kept in solitary confinement.

By torchlight we were amazed to see that the whitewashed walls were covered with graffiti and as we peered at the messages, Allan, Laura and Lauren were surprised to discover just how much had been scribed by Scottish POWs. The messages were varied – some were insulting to their captors, others amusing (one described how he was in confinement for drinking too much beer!) but many were moving and deeply poignant.

It was a remarkable legacy that had been preserved for over seventy years and as much had been written in pencil the survival of their writing is even more extraordinary. Now, with the dedication of Piotr and others, those messages are being carefully recorded before they disappear forever.

26. POW cartoon drawings from Fort XI.

In the grounds of the fort we scrambled up to the gun platforms, viewed ammunition stores, trudged through wooded areas and saw where the remnants of Red Cross parcel contents could still be found. We could have spent much longer exploring and soaking up the atmosphere, but it was time to return to the city centre. We had one last visit to make.

A short walk from the centre of Toruń takes you to Grudziądzka Street and the local cemetery where some British POWs who died in captivity had been interred. Dad's photographs showed the coffins

27. POW burial at cemetery in Toruń.

28. POW burial procession at cemetery in Toruń.

draped with Union Jack flags, being carried to the graveside by fellow POWs and accompanied by German guards. *The Geneva Convention* (Article 76) states that 'belligerents shall ensure that prisoners of war who have died in captivity are honourably buried.'[4]

We had taken the funeral procession photos that we had found among Dad's memorabilia with us to Toruń and as we walked through the cemetery Lauren noticed that many of the gravestones and pathways were still recognisable from these old photos. Looking closely, we were now able to accurately pinpoint where one POW graveside ceremony had taken place. It gave us a strong sense of connection to the past but also a feeling of sadness as we remembered an unknown British POW who had died in prison far from home and family.

A simple cross and a number marked one grave, but it is unlikely that it is now the resting place of a British POW as after hostilities ended the bodies of Allied POWs were exhumed from local cemeteries across Poland and laid to rest in Malbork (formerly Marienburg) Commonwealth War Cemetery. Of the 232 men buried there the largest number came from Toruń.[5]

We do not know if our Dad had ever considered going back to visit Toruń. Up until the late 1980s Poland was a satellite state of the Soviet Union and it was only in 1991 that a peaceful transition to democracy began. Although travel to Poland may then have become easier, by this time most of the surviving prisoners from the World War Two prison camps in German occupied Poland, like our Dad, were well into their seventies.

Although we had seen so much in our short visit, we knew we had only touched the surface. 'There is much more I could tell you,' said Piotr when we parted company. We had experienced the living history of the former POW camp and our time in Toruń had made a deep and lasting impression. Yet by the time we left we felt, not just sadness, but a sense of peace.

Although Dad himself may not have returned to visit Stalag XXA, we felt that his spirit had been with us. Exactly seventy-two years before, on Thursday 9 April 1942, he had written in his diary,

> *Very warm and pleasant these days – started work in library today – Alan Moore went to Fort 14. Wrote postcard home and one to Auto Club.*

Twelve

The Drottningholm

October 1943 to March 1992

The abrupt end of diary entries in March 1943 led us to re-examine Dad's service records and to discover that in October 1943 he had been selected for repatriation to the United Kingdom.

We do not know how much notice prisoners were given about the repatriation plans but those selected must scarcely have been able to believe the good news. The war had not yet ended and only a few POWs would have this opportunity to return home. Most POWs at Stalag XXA had to wait until the war was drawing to a close in early 1945 for their chance for freedom. In the final weeks of the conflict they were made to march west across Poland in the depths of a severe winter. Those who survived finally became free men when the war ended in Europe in May 1945.

The *Geneva Convention* contained Articles (68 and 69) relating to the repatriation of wounded soldiers and long-term POWs and right from the start of World War Two the ICRC carried out negotiations between Britain and Germany for a protected ferry service and hospital ships to be used for repatriation exchanges. Plans for an exchange between British and German POWs, with the participation of the German Government, was finally arranged for 20 October

1943. The agreement was for British and Commonwealth POWs held in German controlled territory to be exchanged in Gothenburg, Sweden, for a similar number of German POWs from UK and Canada. Included in over 4000 British POWs were a large number of the sick and wounded, 'protected personnel' (which included medical staff) as well as civilian internees and merchant seamen. [1]

Both Alistair MacRitchie and Archie Dey were also selected for this repatriation party and although Alan Moore had been due to return home at this time as well, he agreed to let someone else take his place and so remained at Stalag XXA.

Alistair's notes show that he was moved back to Stalag XXA on the 15 October where he was happy to be once more reunited with his close friends as well as others from the 153 Field Ambulance. The following day, Saturday 16 October, the repatriation party left the camp. The first stage of their twenty-two-hour long journey, once again on cattle trucks, took them via the town of Stettin in north-west Poland (now called Szczecin) before eventually reaching the Baltic port of Sassnitz in northern Germany on 17 October. Here they were transferred on to one of the waiting train ferries for the sea crossing to Trelleborg in Sweden. [2] An electric train took them on the final leg to Gothenburg arriving in the early hours of 18 October 1943 - Dad's twenty-fifth birthday.

The British POWs were put on board the liner *Drottningholm* which was docked at the harbour in Gothenburg and waited there for a day or two until all arrangements for the exchange had been confirmed. The TS *Drottningholm* was a transatlantic ocean liner owned by the Swedish American Line. During the Second World War she was used by the British and French as a repatriation mercy ship and for these voyages she had the word 'Protected' painted on her sides. We know that Dad was definitely on the *Drottningholm* on 18 October because he wrote a postcard to his mother.

When the time came to sail, most of the British men were transferred on to the troopship *Empress of Russia* which commenced its sea voyage to Britain on 21 October. The *RMS Empress of Russia* was an ocean liner built by Fairfield Shipbuilding & Engineering Company at

29. Drottningholm postcard front and reverse.

Govan in Glasgow, Scotland for the Canadian Pacific Railway. She regularly sailed the trans-Pacific route between Canada and the Far East. During World War Two she was commissioned by the British

Admiralty as a troop transport and in 1941-42 Midshipman Philip Mountbatten (who became the now late Duke of Edinburgh) was a member of the crew. In October 1943 the vessel was also used for the exchange of POWs from Gothenburg.[3]

Three ships in total, carrying over 4000 repatriates, were escorted by German destroyers around the northern tip of Jutland and out into the North Sea. At an agreed point off the Norwegian coast, the German destroyers turned back and the British RAF Coastal Command took over the escort duty.[4]

The sea journey lasted several days and on 25 October 1943 the *Empress of Russia* finally docked at Leith. Dad was back on British soil and no longer a POW.

On arrival, the newly repatriated men were welcomed home by Sir William Darling, at that time the Lord Provost of Edinburgh. Bands playing music were there to greet them as they disembarked. A newspaper cutting found among Dad's memorabilia shows General Sir Ronald Adam reading the King's message to the men as they crowded together to listen. Both Dad and Alistair can clearly be seen amongst the group of men, near the centre of the photograph. The caption for the photograph read: 'The first batch of repatriated prisoners of war arrive in Leith: General Sir Ronald Adam, Adjutant-General to the forces, reading out a message of cordial greetings from the King and Queen.'

'The Queen and I bid you a very warm welcome. Your trials and sufferings have constantly been in our thoughts. We rejoice that you are safely home, even though the actual homes to some of you are in distant parts.

With all our hearts we hope that your release from captivity will bring you restored health and a full measure of happiness.'

The King's Message [5]

A Pathé Newsreel from the time entitled 'Home Sweet Home' shows similar scenes and again we were able to pick out both Dad and Alistair standing together in the crowd. General Sir Ronald Adam is heard speaking to the men and there is footage of the military bands playing on the quayside. Although efforts were clearly made to provide a welcome homecoming for the men it seems unlikely the celebratory atmosphere extended beyond the dockside. At this stage the war was ongoing, men were still fighting on the front lines and the repatriated POWs probably did not feel they were returning to their country as heroes.

Each man received a letter whilst still on board the ship explaining what would happen on their immediate return as well as details on pay, issue of new uniforms and so on. According to this document they were permitted to send a postcard to relatives whilst still on board ship (most likely this is Dad's Drottningholm postcard). In addition, they could send a free telegram to family to let them know they had arrived safely in the UK but there was no possibility of relatives being allowed to greet them:

> 'On arrival in England those of you who have to go to hospital will be transferred direct to ambulance trains which will be waiting alongside. The rest of you will be taken by train to a Service Establishment. There will, therefore, be no opportunity for your relatives and friends to greet you at the port of disembarkation.
>
> On arrival you will be taken to a Service Establishment where you will be kept as short a time as possible before going on leave.'[6]

Left: 30. Close up detail of Dad and Alistair arriving at Leith. The Illustrated London News, October 1943.

Next page: 31. Repatriates arriving at Leith. The Illustrated London News, October 1943.

Dad's service and casualty form shows that the day after arrival at Leith he was at 'C' Company, 1st Depot RAMC. All Army and RAF personnel were then given 28 days leave.

The repatriated men were however under strict instructions about what they were allowed to talk about regarding their time as POWs and were required to sign showing they had understood the document. Anyone found breaking any of the rules would be subject to disciplinary action.

News of the repatriates' arrival in Leith was reported in newspapers the following day, 26 October 1943.

> 'Repatriated prisoners of war, who include some men of the 51st Division from Inverness, Beauly and Nairn, were disembarked at Leith yesterday… Embarkation from the ships in the Forth was carried out by a fleet of tenders which brought their excited passengers to the quayside at intervals throughout the day. At the quayside the arrivals were given a tremendous reception, and later were conveyed by rail and road to various medical centres in the United Kingdom.'[7]

> *Inverness Courier*, 26 October 1943

Throughout the following days and weeks, the *Inverness Courier* printed various articles about repatriated men who had returned to the Highland area and described how some were met with pipers and a huge welcoming crowd at Inverness Railway Station.

Our aunt Jean told us that they had not known when Dad was getting home to Inverness and the family had travelled to Broughty Ferry to visit his older sister Milly and her husband Harry who was stationed there. She recalls that Dad had made his way home to Inverness only to find no-one at the house. A neighbour explained to him that his mother and sister were away, and so he decided to travel back south to surprise them. As he was boarding the bus in Dundee to go to Broughty Ferry he noticed a woman already seated who looked very familiar. It turned out to be his mother!

WARNING AGAINST GIVING INFORMATION WHICH MAY BE OF

VALUE TO THE ENEMY [8]

(This applies to members of all Services and continues even after discharge therefrom)

1.   It is the duty of all persons to safeguard information which might be useful, directly or indirectly, to the enemy. Such information includes details of any attempted or premeditated escapes, and information of a secret nature of which a Prisoner of War may have obtained knowledge whilst in captivity.

2.   The Defence Regulations make it an Offence, punishable with imprisonment, to publish or to communicate to any unauthorised person any information or anything which purports to be information or any matter which would or might be directly or indirectly useful to the enemy.

3.   Information regarding attempted or premeditated escapes, as well as information of a secret nature of which you have obtained knowledge whilst in captivity, should be communicated only to a representative of M.I.9 War Office and persons authorised by M.I.9 to interview you later.

4.   When writing back to P.W. it is prohibited to refer to naval, military, serial, economic or political matters, movements of troops or ships. No mention is to be made of any matters likely to attach suspicion to the P.W. or prejudice his position in any way in the eyes of the enemy.

5.   If you are asked by representatives of British Red Cross Society or of the Press to give a description of your experiences as a P.W. you are to confine yourself strictly to welfare matters such as food, clothing, educational, religious or recreational facilities. Nothing is to be said that might react unfavourably to other P.W. or mislead relatives of P.W.

I have read this warning and understand that I shall be liable to disciplinary action if I disclose to anyone information of the kind mentioned above.

Date............................   Signed ....

When they were all back home in Inverness a family meal was arranged to celebrate the homecoming and Dad's ex-colleague and friend Kathleen Tait was invited as a guest. The meal at Dochfour Drive was a quiet celebration with no fuss or fanfare.

Returning to military duties once more must have been an anti-climax for Dad and others like him. Perhaps he wondered about the friends and fellow POWs still in captivity back in Poland, maybe he even felt guilty to have been one of the lucky ones to get home.

As a former POW Dad could not be sent overseas again and his documents were stamped:

> 'Repatriated under the Geneva Convention –
> employment restricted to medical units in a non-
> combatant capacity. Not to be sent overseas before 25
> April 1944'.

Dad perhaps had no interest in continuing his army career as a nursing orderly as his service record shows that in January 1944, three months after his return to Britain, he was placed on the waiting list for training as a clerk which commenced at the Military Hospital Fort George, near Inverness, towards the end of April 1944. By 20 August of that year he was listed as 'graded and mustered Clerk Group 'C' Class III' and relinquishing mustering as nursing orderly on the same date. This was signed by Captain Makepeace, 13 Company RAMC. A year later, on 30 August 1945 he advanced to Clerk Group 'C' Class II.

Hostilities finally came to an end in Europe in September 1945 and by February 1946 Dad was shown as posted to 'Y' list and at the beginning of June was released to Class 'Z' (T) Royal Army Reserve. Finally, on 30 June 1959, he was discharged from Reserve Liability under the Navy, Army and Air Forces Reserve Act 1959.

On his 1946 Release Leave Certificate the Commanding Officer wrote:

> *'A highly intelligent and competent man...... He (Allan Cameron) was unfortunately taken prisoner early in the war and in consequence did not obtain that military advancement that was his undoubted due. Absolutely reliable and hardworking. A really first class man.'*

Back home

After his discharge in 1946, our father began to pick up the threads of his life, determined not to let the war define his future. He did not resume his law apprenticeship in Inverness but instead moved to Glasgow to complete a business studies course at the Glasgow and West of Scotland Commercial College and in the years following he worked with various well-known food and drink companies. In September1949 he was supervising a sales team with 40 members and 30 vans covering a widespread area of central Scotland – Ayr, Kilmarnock, Greenock and Edinburgh. In his spare time, he enjoyed visits to the theatre and also maintained his interest in playing table tennis as he had in Stalag XXA.

32. Alistair and Helen MacRitchie at
Mum and Dad's wedding, April 1952.

Having made a life for himself in Glasgow, it was here that Dad eventually met our mother, Euphemia McCallum (known as Effie or Fay) and on 2 April 1952 they were married at Queens Park Baptist Church in Glasgow. Alistair MacRitchie was also settled in Glasgow by this time and the two friends remained close. Through reading

33. Mum and Dad's wedding day, April 1952.

Alistair's memoirs, we discovered they had also been 'best men' at each other's weddings!

In 1963 our family moved north to the seaside town of Nairn, fifteen miles from Inverness, and bought a large property for the purpose of running a guest house. Nairn was an obvious choice as it was close to where Dad had been brought up and near Bunchrew where our mother had been billeted during the war when she was with the WAAF (Women's Auxiliary Air Force). It was also familiar territory for us as every year we holidayed on our aunt and uncle's farm at Fleenasmore on the outskirts of Nairn. Add to that the town's reputation as 'Brighton of the North' and its popularity as a seaside holiday destination, it was the ideal place to run a bed and breakfast business.

Once we were established in Nairn and the house had been suitably decorated and furnished, our mother took charge of running the bed and breakfast business at 'Janefield' in Waverley Road during the summer months. Dad resumed his interest in accountancy and law and for a number of years worked with the solicitor's firm of Donaldson & Henderson. At weekends Dad helped out in the guest house when it was particularly busy.

Those early years in Nairn were happy and exciting times for all of us. As children we were thrilled to have the run of the house, a cellar, numerous outbuildings, and a spacious garden while Mum and Dad were able to enjoy holidays and cruises abroad at the end of the summer season. Some guests, like Nancy and Tom Millar and their children Lesley and David, visited Nairn and 'Janefield' on more than one occasion. Over the years the Millar's became close family friends and to this day we still keep in touch with Lesley.

The quieter lifestyle seemed to suit Dad and in his spare time he enjoyed fishing and walking along the seafront. He also still enjoyed an occasional game of table tennis and was a keen member and regular attender of the Nairn Bridge Club. Our Mum was a member of the Nairn Old Parish Church and became involved with the Women's Guild and the Toc H Christian voluntary movement.

There had always been the hope when we moved north that the

drier climate of the Moray Firth area would be beneficial to Dad's health. Leaving the damp and smog of Glasgow may have helped but he continued to suffer from chest problems and eventually emphysema was diagnosed. In 1970, after Dad was widowed, we moved house, although he continued to live and work in Nairn. Eventually he remarried and Alistair MacRitchie was again his best man. Sadly, Dad's health continued to deteriorate over the years and in 1992 he unexpectedly suffered a heart attack and died aged only seventy-three years.

34. Fiona, Dad and Carole early 1980's.

Thirteen

Full Circle

May 2014 to June 2015

In June, not long after returning from Toruń, we received an e-mail from Stuart in Canada with an attached message. It said,

'I am Archie Dey's daughter, Heather...'

Having resigned ourselves to the likelihood that we would never find out anything about Archie's post war life and that the story of the third 'musketeer' would forever remain untold, this was an extraordinary and astonishing piece of good news. Through an unexpected chain of events, the close association of the three men and their wartime bond had eventually helped us to track each other down.

While researching her family history Heather had emailed Stuart after coming across Alistair's memoirs by chance while browsing on the internet. Stuart was then able to pass on the news to us and to tell Heather that he and George were also in touch with Allan Cameron's daughters and that remarkably we had all met up with Alan Moore who had known Alistair, our father and Heather's father Archie when they were POWs in Stalag XXA.

Before we heard from Heather there were already plans in place for the Camerons and the MacRitchies to meet up again later in the year. We had arranged to get together in Nairn around late August to coincide with Stuart and Velma's next visit to the UK. By luck the date we had chosen suited Heather and her husband David and, although it was short notice, within days they had managed to organise flights up from London to join us. Again, it seemed that good fortune was on our side.

Alan was delighted to hear that Archie's daughter had been in touch with Stuart but unfortunately a trip to join us in Scotland was now too much of an undertaking. However, Alan was at last able to speak to Heather on the phone to hear what had happened to Archie after the war and to share his memories of the times they had spent together as POWs.

In the weeks leading up to our meeting we had time to exchange photos and information and Heather had the opportunity to read Alistair's memoirs. During the four years between November 1939 and October 1943, we knew from our Dad's diaries that Archie and Dad had been together for at least two and a half years, as part of the 51st and later as fellow POWs.

When we finally got together on Saturday 22 August 2014 it was just weeks short of seventy-five years since Dad, Alistair and Archie had first met. Like us, Heather had grown up hearing her father mention the names of his wartime friends and had also come across a copy of 'The Three Musketeers' wartime photo showing Archie, Alistair and Dad in their RAMC uniforms.

We discovered that Archie had been born and brought up in Glasgow and was a Glaswegian 'through and through.' Like Dad and Alistair, he had talked little about the conflict but had once spoken about 'lying in ditches with the dead and wounded all around' – a description that echoes what our Dad had once recounted and what Alistair had written in his memoirs. Although we cannot be completely certain, we feel sure that Dad and Archie had been the 'pals' who had volunteered to join Alistair on the ambulance convoy that was ambushed while heading to St Valery.

After the war, Archie had returned to visit Stalag XXA and St Valery and on his return from Normandy had written to the Commonwealth War Graves Commission to enquire about two of his friends who had been in the 153 FA. The Commission confirmed that Private David Williams and Private George McCulloch, both aged twenty, had died on 11 June 1940 - the day before the 51st Highland Division were captured. Sadly, there are no known graves but both men are commemorated by name on the Dunkirk Memorial in France.

35. Archie Dey and Dad

Archie was a fan of pipe band music. He played the drums and was never without his drumsticks. When we showed Heather a grey knitted body warmer of Dad's from his time as a POW, we learned that Archie had also been a dab hand at knitting. We had always assumed that the body warmer had been sent from home and posted out in a 'next of kin' parcel but now there was a possibility that it may very well have been the results of Archie's handiwork!

From our Dad's diaries we knew that during his time in captivity Archie had twice been transported to other camps. On one occasion, according to Dad's notes on February 1943, Archie had been detailed to work in a camp around seventy miles north of Toruń called Marienburg or Stalag XXB as it was also known.

During his time in Marienburg Archie had met and become firm friends with a fellow Scot who turned out to be Dad's post-war friend Johnnie McComiskey. On one occasion Johnnie had risked severe punishment himself in order to help Archie. After an attempted escape, Archie had been put in solitary confinement and it was Johnnie who slid food under his cell door to help keep him alive.

Eventually Archie was returned to Stalag XXA before finally being repatriated in October 1943. As Archie had met Johnnie while he was at Stalag XXB, it seems likely that Dad and Johnnie had met and become firm friends after the war due to their connection to Archie and their shared experiences of being captured at St Valery and becoming prisoners of war.

When Archie returned to the UK, he was sent to Buchanan Castle in Drymen as a medical orderly and after the war spent most of his working life abroad in various far-flung locations. Heather was able to tell us that once his position with the Control Commission in Germany had ended, her father worked in Kent before setting sail for Canada where he spent almost three years before returning to the UK. Archie then completed six overseas Foreign Office postings. While on 'home leave' Archie always returned to Scotland and on his retiral settled in Irvine, Ayrshire, where Johnnie McComiskey at that time also lived. They visited each other every week and remained close lifelong friends.

None of us know for certain whether Archie had ever met up with our Dad or Alistair after their return to the UK. While living in Canada, Dad and Archie may have corresponded and Heather thought it was possible that one of Archie's brothers may even have met up with either Dad or Alistair on a number of occasions.

Archie's service book and medals survived but sadly no other paperwork relating to his time during the war has come to light. However, a substantial collection of wartime newspaper cuttings had been carefully preserved by Archie's mother. It proved to be a fascinating record and timeline of what had happened to the men of the 51st during the war years.

Various articles report concerns about the welfare and treatment of the British POWs including government statements given by Mr Anthony Eden, War Minister. From November 1943 accounts in local newspapers mention Archie's safe return home and echo the intense

36. Back row from left: Stuart MacRitchie, George MacRitchie. Front row from left: Carole Grant, Fiona Cameron, Heather French.

emotions and immense relief felt by many families.

It was an afternoon which none of us had imagined would ever have taken place as we reminisced and swapped stories about Archie's, Alistair's and our Dad's experiences during their army training days through to repatriation and beyond. Both fascinating and poignant at times there was no doubt that together the three of them had witnessed many tragic events in France and when imprisoned had gone through dark and dire times. Yet, during some of their most difficult and testing times it was reassuring to know that during the war years Alistair, Archie and Dad had the companionship of others alongside their close friendship as 'The Three Musketeers.'

September - December 2014

On 23 September an article about how our Dad's wartime connection had led to our families making contact was published in the *Inverness Courier*. Included in the article were our own thoughts on how Alistair, Archie and our Dad might have reacted to the news that their families had all met.

Stuart felt his father would have been 'surprised' to know that we had all managed to find each other while Heather explained that her father had always looked to the future rather than the past but added, 'That said, I think he would be amazed and actually rather chuffed.'[1] Fiona and I were sure that Dad would have been thrilled to know we had all met up and would have loved hearing how the story unfolded.

Reflecting on their time during the war years George said: 'I'm sure they had the occasional good time but from the time they were captured till they were repatriated it was pretty grim and they tried not to think about it once they got home.'[2]

Just when we thought we had discovered everything we were ever likely to know about Dad, Archie and Alistair we came across some old items of family correspondence. A letter written to Dad by his mother in the 1950s showed that Archie's and Dad's families had remained in touch years after the end of the war. In the incomplete and only letter we have from that time our grandmother writes,

> '...I had a very nice letter from Mrs Dey and she told me that Archie ... left for Canada last Sept: ... They settled in Toronto and Archie got a good job, but Mrs Dey did not say what he was doing...'

Our second find was messages of condolences which had been sent to the family after our father passed away. While sorting out our stepmothers' effects we had come across cards and letters from Dad's long-time friends. Along with a sympathy card from Johnnie there were two handwritten letters from Alistair and a message from Archie.

When Alistair wrote to our stepmother in 1992, he said,

> '... irrespective of time I still have vivid memories of wartime in France and in Poland and in peacetime. We were good and close friends...'

While in a separate letter to us Alistair explained how and where their friendship had begun and endured.

> 'I first met your father over 52 years ago in a barrack room in the South of England and whether because of him coming from Inverness, and me from Fort William, we became firm friends, along with Archie Dey from Glasgow.
>
> We have not seen each other for quite some time but nothing will eradicate the long and vivid memories of our friendship.
>
> I have no knowledge of the whereabouts of Archie Dey and I mention him as he was one of the 'Three Musketeers' during the war...'
>
> Sincerely yours
>
> Alistair MacRitchie. (11th March 1992)

And from Archie, whom we had never met but who had known Dad so well as a young man, his sentiments were expressed in these

few words,

> 'Allan was my closest pal throughout our war years and a wonderful comrade.
>
> God bless you,
>
> Archie'

37. Reflections from Toruń, Rod Butler. Original ceramic tile created by Rod Butler, 2015.

June 2015

Our Dad had never spoken about Saint Valery-en-Caux. It was
only from his war records, a brief diary entry and a postcard
that we learned of his capture on June 12 1940. The card featured
a harbour and sea views from St Valery-en-Caux but the date and
postmark were too blurred to read. From the address we knew it must
have been sent in the 60s and the signature showed it had been written
by Johnnie McComiskey.

> 'This will bring back some memories to you Allan - it has
> to me! The Mem. [Memorial] Stone to the 51st H/Div is
> on the right. The whole harbour area is unrecognisable
> being completely rebuilt.
>
> Regards to all. H (Helen) & Johnnie'

When we met up with Heather in Nairn, we were very interested to
hear about the 75th anniversary of the capture of the 51st HD at St
Valery-en-Caux which she and her family were planning to attend in
2015. We had often talked about the possibility of visiting St Valery-
en-Caux and when Heather contacted us again in May of that year, we
made the snap decision to go. St Valery-en-Caux and Veules-les-
Roses had organised a three-day programme to mark the 75th
anniversary of the events of June 1940.

Five weeks later on the morning of 11 June we left Inverness for St
Valery-en-Caux in France. We were looking forward to our trip but
with only one day to get there it was a tight schedule, and we were
anxious about arriving in time. All went to plan until an unexpected
train delay meant that we would be arriving late in Yvetot and would
miss the last bus connection to St Valery-en-Caux.

We contacted our Airbnb host to explain that we would be arriving
later than planned. To our surprise and relief, he offered to come and
meet us at Yvetot. We had just enough time for a look around the
station where Dad, as part of the BEF, had arrived by train and left 'by
lorry' on his first day in France.

185

The thirty-minute drive from Yvetot to St Valery-en-Caux took us through peaceful farmland. How different the landscape must have looked when the Division, under attack by the German forces, was retreating to St Valery-en-Caux hoping for evacuation by sea. Somewhere along those roads was the ditch where Dad and his pals and injured soldiers had taken cover when ambushed and fired upon on 11 June. It was also near here where their forced march into captivity as POWs began.

We arrived at our accommodation after our host gave us an impromptu tour of the main sights of St Valery-en-Caux. As the coastal town is now a popular seaside holiday resort, finding a bed for two nights had been difficult but any misgivings we might have had about our last-minute booking were unfounded.

Our studio flat was spacious, comfortable and in a quiet but central location. Unscathed by the war the traditional house and outbuildings had been in the family for two generations. Although tired, during the night ominous cracks of thunder and flashes of lightening disturbed our sleep. In the wee small hours, we imagined the distant storm was echoing the clatter of explosions and heavy gunfire from seventy-five years before.

It was a fresh clear morning when we set out towards the town centre and it did not take us long to discover the charms of St Valery-en-Caux. The town which had originated in Roman times now has a busy marina crammed with pleasure boats and a scattering of fishing vessels. Walking along Avenue Foch we reached the main square. It was market day and stalls were overflowing with local produce and freshly caught fish as we headed towards the beach to see the spectacular white cliffs which we had heard so much about.

To reach the cliff tops on foot involves a fairly steep climb but our aim was to reach the summit around mid-morning to mark the time when Dad and his comrades had been captured. The cliff face seemed untouched by the past until we noticed the discreet remains of a disused bunker built into the stone, part of the Atlantic Wall fortifications from World War Two. Climbing upwards the steps abruptly came to a halt as the path fanned out towards a sloped grassy area.

It is here on the high east cliff of St Valery-en-Caux, the Falaises d'Amont, where the proud memorial dedicated to the men of the 51st Highland Division stands. It was unveiled in June 1950 and was made from granite shipped over from Inver Quarry in Aberdeenshire. At around five metres tall the memorial, which is centred on a Celtic cross, commands a panoramic view over the town. On the opposite cliff, the Falaise d'Aval, is a memorial stone to commemorate the French Cavalry who fell defending St Valery-en-Caux in June 1940.

Flower beds edge the path leading up to the HD monument where an inscription simply says, 'In proud and grateful memory of all ranks of the 51st HD who gave their lives during the war 1939-45.' A second legend in Gaelic reads, 'La a bhlair is math na cairdean' (On the day of battle it is good to have friends.) In preparation for the evening ceremony the Scottish Saltire, the Union Jack and the French Tricolour had been raised. We paused to reflect before heading up towards the clifftops.

To the east side of the Pays de Caux plateau, ripening wheat fields stretched for miles along the flat exposed coastline and swept inland. Any buildings were indistinct shapes in the distance and out to sea there was a hazy blue horizon. Exactly where Dad was captured we shall never know but as we walked along the narrow path hugging the cliff edge, we knew that it must have been nearby.

From 1940 photographs of the clifftop area, little seems to have changed over the years. The sea-views would still be recognisable and it was easy to see how the dramatic chalk cliffs had played their part in the tragic fate of the 51st. One signpost warned of the dangers of going too close to the edge and glancing through the undergrowth we could see the sheer drop to the stony beach below where many men had perished on that day. Looking towards the Channel, for a few precious moments Dad was with us on that breezy morning as we stood and gazed out across the sea. Wildflowers were scattered in the rough grass beside broken stumps of concrete fences. We stopped and slipped two red poppies inside our notebook.

Retracing our steps back towards the memorial stone we saw that a

38. Cliffs at St Valery-en-Caux, June 2015

group of around twenty people had gathered. English was being spoken and we listened as memoirs written by British soldiers who had been captured at St Valery-en-Caux were read aloud.

It was moving to hear the words of survivors being spoken seventy-five years to the day, time and place when the 51st were forced to surrender and we thought of Dad, Alistair, Archie and Alan. We recalled Alistair's descriptions of their capture and Alan's account of how desperate it had been for him and many others as they had tried to escape down the cliffs using makeshift ropes.

As the group at the memorial began to disperse, we approached and introduced ourselves. One of the party turned out to be Captain Charles Grant of 7 SCOTS. 7 SCOTS are an infantry unit of Territorials and although they did not exist in 1940 most of their antecedent units, such as the Black Watch and the Camerons, were in the 51st Division. Today they are a Reserve Battalion of the Royal Regiment of Scotland. The group were on a battlefield tour of the area visiting important sites connected with the 51st's withdrawal from the Somme to St Valery-en-Caux. We were delighted when they asked us to join them for the next part of that day's itinerary.

Making our way back down to the market square everyone gathered close to the spot where on 12 June Major General Fortune surrendered to Generalmajor Rommel. An iconic photograph of that moment shows the two men standing side by side while burnt-out buildings smoulder in the background. Eighty per cent of the town had been destroyed.

Extracts were read from books and poignant speeches made as we stood in the town square. But it was the description of the impact that surrender had on the morale of the Scottish troops that we remember vividly. When men from the Black Watch were given orders by Major Thomas Rennie to cease fire and surrender, for most of them the unthinkable had happened. Eric Linklater describes in his book *The Highland Division*, how no-one could at first believe the order that had been given. As the hoplessness of the situation became apparent, many accounts tell of how the men felt both angry and humiliated and some wept.

Many in the battlefield tour group were visibly moved as everyone stood in silence while a lone piper played. Capture was not what the men of the 51st had been prepared for. Their fate was to be years of hardship and imprisonment and for the citizens of St Valery-en-Caux it was the beginning of over four long years of German occupation.

Later that day we walked towards the outskirts of the town to see the St Valery-en-Caux Franco-British War Cemetery. On the way we paid a visit to the Church of St Joseph to see the commemorative window that had been gifted to the people of St Valery-en-Caux from Inverness and the towns of Scotland in 1990. The imagery of the stained-glass window depicts an aerial landscape showing the position of the allied forces and the movement of the German army in 1940. Scottish thistles and French roses are symbolically entwined to represent the joint action of the French army and the 51st Highland Division.

Approaching the cemetery from the Avenue D'Ecosse we were surprised to see a familiar sight. A local tour bus from Buckie, a town close to our home in Nairn, was parked outside. The coach had brought a tour group from the Western Isles. Before long we were sharing our thoughts about Stalag XXA and St Valery-en-Caux with the parents of Norman MacArthur who, with Piotr from Toruń, had featured in the recent From Stalag to Gulag television documentary.

In the immaculately kept grounds men from all divisions and ranks of the French infantry and the Highland Division, who had died defending St Valery-en-Caux had been laid to rest.

Altogether there are 218 French military burials and 234 British and Commonwealth graves. In the centre stands the Cross of Sacrifice with the St Andrew's shield set into its base. Names etched on the headstones of the British graves reflect the Highland ancestry of many of them and in this section also lie sixty-three graves which are marked 'Known unto God.' Beside two unnamed headstones we laid wooden crosses and poppies. Weeks later when we spoke to Alan about St Valery-en-Caux, it was photographs of the cemetery that brought back to him the most emotional and vivid memories of fallen comrades.

That evening we once again made our way up to the HD memorial and stood alongside Archie's daughter Heather and her family to watch the official ceremony. We were met by a colourful scene of red, white and blue as flag bearers positioned themselves alongside the Highland Division Normandy and the Normandy Highland Pipe Band. Dignitaries from France and Scotland with sashes and chains of honour were congregating while re-enactment soldiers from France 44 dressed in authentic 1940 uniforms gathered close to the memorial.

Deputee-Maire Dominique Chauvel spoke passionately about the importance of never forgetting the past and of how the people of St Valery-en-Caux will always remember the British soldiers and especially those of the 51st who fought alongside the French. It was a moving and uniting tribute.

39. HD memorial on clifftop at St Valery-en-Caux, June 2015.

40. St Valery-en-Caux Franco-British Cemetery, June 2015.

At the ceremony there was official representation from the Highlands with the Inverness Provost Alec Graham giving an address in Gaelic. Wreaths were laid, the pipe band played, and another brief deluge of rain did nothing to spoil the spirit of the occasion. It was a privilege and honour to be able to join in the ceremony alongside other British and French citizens in this act of remembrance.

In the centre of the gathering was a poignant reminder of why we had made the journey to St Valery-en-Caux. A ninety-four-year-old veteran of the 51st, from Cambuslang in Scotland, had made the visit with his family. We thought of Alan whose health had prevented him from making the journey but who too would be remembering this day. As the ceremony came to a close everyone present was invited by the mayor to attend a reception in the town hall. It was to take place in the Salle d'Ecosse.

Aptly named, the room is large and airy with a distinct Highland flavour. A Scottish themed mural covers one wall and a collection of photographs gifted from Inverness are displayed on another. A cabinet containing regimental memorabilia and two kilted mannequins also have their place. 'Glasses of Friendship' were shared, and as guest of honour, the Scottish veteran was presented with gifts of gratitude from the people of St Valery-en-Caux.

Two days later we were waiting for the early morning bus back to Yvetot. The town was beginning to stir as occasional cyclists crisscrossed the main junction. Beside the bus stop there was a wartime memorial plaque set into the wall. It was in memory of American soldiers who had died in a tragic accident at St Valery-en-Caux on the 17th January 1945. Brake failure on the steep hill leading down into the town had caused a packed train to career out of control and crash through the station building. Around 85 American troops were believed to have been killed while many others were seriously injured. Although the station re-opened after the tragedy it finally closed for good in 1996. The people of St Valery-en-Caux had ensured that the loss of Allied lives in whatever circumstances would be remembered.

As we headed along the Avenue de 51st Highland Division towards

Yvetot it seemed far too soon to be leaving. Although our early morning departure meant we would miss the parade and services at the Colonel Labouche Monument and the Military Cemetery we had been fortunate to be able to attend other important commemorative events on the previous day.

On our first day in St Valery-en-Caux, we by chance met Freda and Rodger Scott from Perth, Scotland. It turned out that they had made the journey to St Valery-en-Caux as Freda's father Jack Kidd, had, like our father, been captured at St Valery-en-Caux and spent many years as a POW. Freda and Rodger had made plans to attend commemoration ceremonies in the surrounding area and kindly invited us to join them on a visit to the nearby coastal village of Veules-les-Roses the next day.

Like St Valery-en-Caux, the picturesque village of Veules-les-Roses had been under intense attack in June 1940 and many men lost their lives as they made desperate attempts to escape. In honour of Captain Derek Lang, 51st Highland Division, who was captured at Veules-les-Roses, an inauguration ceremony to officially open a cliffside path in his name had been organised. Processions including pipe bands marched through the village to where the Sente du Capitaine Derek Lang (Captain Derek Lang Trail) was opened by his daughter. Relatives of Captain Derek Lang were also present at the cliff top Canon Memorial as plaques to commemorate fallen British and French soldiers were unveiled. Late in the afternoon, white balloons representing all those who had lost their lives were released into the sky by local school children.

On our last evening we met Heather and her husband David to enjoy some French food and wine together at a local restaurant. We were also delighted to have the company of Heather's son Ross and his partner Sarah. Both keen cyclists, they were planning to extend their stay and follow the first part of the route which the POWs, including Archie, were forced to march as they headed for Poland. As we shared family memories of our fathers and reminisced about our visit it was a perfect ending to our stay in St Valery-en-Caux.

Most people we had met in Normandy had come for personal

reasons. Many were from the generation of sons and daughters like us who had grown up knowing little or nothing about their fathers' experiences during the war but who were keen to find out more. However, after seventy-five years, what took place at St Valery-en-Caux still divides opinion. Some historians have analysed the complex political and military background to the events at St Valery-en-Caux with many being critical of Churchill's role, while others refute this. Whatever the reasons, the dramatic evacuation of 300,000 soldiers at Dunkirk has rightly continued to be seen as a success but the 'embarrassment' of capture at St Valery-en-Caux has been largely forgotten.

St Valery-en-Caux may have been seen by some as a military disaster but the 51st had put up a determined fight. Hundreds lost their lives, thousands were injured, and many more thousands captured. Numerous accounts of acts of heroism have been retold and today it is felt by some that those stories and the fate of the 51st deserve to be recognised.

As we left St Valery-en-Caux, we felt proud of the spirit and discipline which the Highland Division had shown in an impossible situation and felt uplifted knowing that each year on 12 June in a corner of Normandy the Division are remembered for their bravery and sacrifice. In a town where street names and memorials are testimony to the fortitude of the Division, they are not forgotten.

In September 1944 the reconstituted 51st Division was given the great honour of liberating St Valery-en-Caux. A 'fellowship' between Inverness and St Valery-en-Caux was formed in February 1945 which later led to their 'twinning' in 1987. Many cultural exchanges have since taken place and plans for future links continue to flourish. In the town of St Valery-en-Caux, the day of liberation and the 51st's involvement is still recognised and remembered.

We had much to reflect on as we travelled back to Paris. Visiting Normandy and seeing where the fate of so many men from the 51st had been sealed helped to make more sense of the past. Meeting others like ourselves and knowing that seventy-five years on those who had been at St Valery-en-Caux were still remembered gave us a sense of pride and optimism for the present and the future. For us, visiting St Valery-en-Caux had brought together and made sense of Dad's unspoken wartime past and our present-day story.

By late morning we had arrived back at the Gard du Nord in good time for our journey to London but the sight of long queues for the Eurostar brought us abruptly back to reality. There was an unexpected delay. An unexploded World War Two device had been detected inside a fellow traveller's suitcase.

Fourteen

Looking Forward

September 2020

Nine years have passed since we first clicked open Dad's battered old suitcase. It had been a fascinating and moving experience as we grew closer to him, met people from the past and got to know the families of those who had known Dad during the war years. Tracing his story had led us to explore the military background of those uncertain and harrowing early days in France and inspired us to visit places we had never heard about.

Thousands who survived the chaos of the fighting in France suffered the humiliation of surrender and had to endure years of captivity. As POWs, meagre rations and hard physical labour were everyday realities and years of imprisonment took its toll mentally. Dad himself wrote about 'going round the bend' as hopes for an early end to captivity failed to materialise. For many, it was contact from home, camaraderie and friendships that sustained them. Religion too played its part. The *Geneva Convention*, although not always adhered to, helped to ensure that, for most of the time, conditions for British prisoners were at least tolerable. Red Cross parcels were essential to their survival, especially in the early days, and ICRC delegate visits gave the men a welcome link to the outside world. Even now, at the former site of Stalag XXA, barbed wire fences and a lookout tower remain as stark reminders of enforced captivity.

The story of St Valery-en-Caux, the capture of the 51st HD and the aftermath still survives today. When Brigadier Grant visited Fort George to talk about the events of 1940, he noted that 2020 would mark the 80th anniversary of the capture of the Division at St Valery-en-Caux although celebratory events had to be postponed. Plans had also been made for a special service to be held on the 75th anniversary of VE day, 8 May 2020, at a new memorial in Toruń to commemorate POWs during and after World War Two.

Closer to home a further unexpected connection between the 153 FA and Dad, Alistair, Archie and Alan came to light. Fiona's partner Iain who is a member of the Army Reserves had recently become Officer Commanding 153 Medical squadron which is part of 225 (Scottish) Medical Regiment. The squadron is based in Dundee and is the direct descendant of the original 153 FA which was in existence in the early 1940s when Dad, Alistair, Archie and Alan were enlisted. After the War, when The Territorial Army was reformed in 1947, the 153 FA underwent significant changes. The 153 (Highland) FA was raised on 1st May 1947 and became part of the 153 (Highland) Brigade, Dundee. In 1967 the TAVR (Territorial and Army Volunteer Reserve) was founded and the Field Ambulance was reduced to a Field Dressing Station. Further changes in 1969 meant the 153 Field Ambulance was retitled 225 (H) Field Ambulance. 225 became a Medical Regiment with squadrons in Dundee, Glenrothes, Sunderland and latterly Stirling.[1]

When we visited Alan and Hilda in 2016, Iain, in his official capacity as Lt Col McIntyre, was able to join us. He presented Alan with an RAMC tie and compiled an article for the RAMC magazine telling Alan's remarkable story. In May 2018 the three of us again visited and Iain recognised Alan's wartime contribution with a plaque from 225 Medical Regiment.

Sadly, Alan passed away in November 2020 at the age of 101. We visited Alan and Hilda in Yorkshire on a number of occasions and over the years we became good friends. Alan was a kind and caring person, always a gentleman and we feel privileged to have known

41. Alan Moore, 19.5.1919 – 14.11.2020

him. We continue to keep in touch with Alan's wife Hilda and hope that future visits to see her may be possible.

We remain in regular contact with Stuart & George MacRitchie and also Archie's daughter Heather who recently told us that she had come across her late uncle's diaries and was pleased to discover that they contained previously unknown details about her own father's experiences during the war years.

In 2017 we also met up with Freda and Rodger Scott in Perth for a personal guided tour of the Black Watch Museum to learn more about

Scotland's oldest Highland regiment and its connection with St Valery-en-Caux. We still keep in touch with Piotr in Toruń.

Up until her death in February 2018, we visited Kathleen Dunlop regularly for afternoon tea. Although our initial connection with Kathleen was through her friendship with Dad, during the course of our visits we got to know her well. She was an engaging companion and we greatly miss her interesting conversation and gentle manner.

42. Kathleen Dunlop, 2018.

Seventy-eight years ago, Dad predicted that 'sometime in the future...' his wartime diaries may be found and read by others perhaps unknown to him. We feel sure that he would have been happy to know that his words sparked our interest and inspired us to look to the future to preserve a small part of his history.

In his diary dated January 1942 he writes, 'May any chance an unauthorised reader scan these pennings...'. Now, as we reflect on how the past and present unexpectedly came together and remember those whom Dad had known as a young man, we feel privileged and fortunate to have been those 'chance readers'.

ALLAN CAMERON

18 October 1918 – 9 March 1992

43. RAMC badge

Private Allan Cameron

RAMC

153 Field Ambulance, 51st Highland Division

HQ Company

British Expeditionary Force

Service Number: 7360345

POW Number 18476

Enlisted:1st November 1939

POW from 12 June 1940 – 25 October 1943

Repatriated to UK: 25 October 1943

Discharged from Reserve liability: 30 June 1959

ACKNOWLEDGEMENTS

We are immensely grateful to all those who helped and encouraged us with *Lemonade Tonight*. Throughout, we have endeavoured to remain true to the recollections of all those who are part of this story. Without their invaluable input, writing this book would not have been possible.

The starting point for us was of course the unexpected discovery of Dad's wartime diaries. We are therefore hugely thankful that our Dad not only kept a record of that dark time in his life so long ago, but also took care to store his diaries safely away in his old suitcase. We count ourselves as incredibly lucky that circumstances allowed us to discover the diaries so many years after the events they described.

To the late Alan Moore we owe a special and heartfelt thank you and we will forever be grateful to have had the immense privilege of listening to his extraordinary story first-hand. Alan's memories of time spent with our father as a prisoner of war were both fascinating and extremely moving. Without the unfailing and willing support of Alan's wife Hilda our opportunity to meet may never have come to pass and for this we are enormously thankful. Their friendship is something we will always treasure.

We owe an unlimited debt to Stuart and George MacRitchie for generously allowing us to use extracts from their father's memoirs. Sincere thanks also to Heather French for sharing many personal memories of her father Archie Dey. We also appreciate the time Alan, Hilda, George, Stuart and Heather took to read, comment on and edit earlier draft extracts.

For initially encouraging us to put pen to paper a special thank you is due to writer James Miller. We are truly appreciative not only of the time he has given us over the years, but also for his endless patience in editing numerous drafts! James's down to earth advice from beginning to end gave us much-needed direction.

Many people gladly helped us over the years, and we are extremely grateful to the following: Freda and Rodger Scott, Dr Peter Duffus, Jean and John Macdonald, Ros Hill, Raphaël Distante, Piotr Olecki, Peter McLoughlin, Peter Pininski, Lyn Nicol, the late Vernon Nicoll and the late Kathleen Dunlop.

Special thanks to Iain McIntyre for providing us with extensive background information about the 153 FA and for reading through draft copies. We are also grateful to our cousins: Mike Morrison for invaluable family details and Sandra McCallum for her much appreciated feedback. Particular thanks go to all those who willingly and freely gave their time to help us successfully research our grandfather's family and WW1 history.

We gratefully acknowledge the help of the many individuals and organisations who assisted and encouraged us during our research including the National Library of Scotland, National Archives, ICRC, CWGC, *Inverness Courier*, British Newspaper Archives, Inverness Local History Forum, British Red Cross, The Gordon Highlanders Museum and the IWM. This list is by no means exhaustive.

For constructive and much needed advice regarding publication we would like to sincerely thank both Duncan Lockerbie and local author Stuart Farrell.

Every effort has been made by us to trace copyright holders and we thank all those who have given advice in this respect. Any errors that remain are our responsibility alone.

Finally, and most of all, to our immediate family we are hugely thankful for their understanding of the time commitment involved, their patience in reading and re-reading drafts and their unfailing encouragement and support throughout.

Fiona Cameron and Carole Grant

Nairn, May 2021

APPENDIX 1: The Thorn Complex (Stalag XXA)

Information from https://www.forces-war-records.co.uk/european-camps-british-commonwealth-prisoners-of-war-1939-45
These forts were all situated on the left bank of the Vistula.

Fort XI (11)
Housed French, British & Polish POWs. Also contained a detention cell.
FORT XII (12)
Soviet prisoners held here before camp at Glinki built
Fort XIII (13)
Housed mainly British POWs
Fort XIV(14)
Camp hospital
Fort XV (15)
Housed mostly British, Australian, New Zealand, Italian and American soldiers.
Fort XVI (16)
Camp prison
Fort XVII (17)
The first camp headquarters (Komendantury Stalag XXA) was in Fort XVII but during the first half of 1940 it was moved to a two-storey house opposite Fort XIII, now known as Okólna Street.
Stalag 312/XXC Glinki
Constructed in second half of 1941 mainly to house large numbers of Soviet POWs. Also accommodated British and Italian prisoners. In the forest between Glinki and Cierpice there is a mass grave where approximately 14,000 Russian POWs are buried.

The Thorn complex was itself a sub-camp of the concentration camp in Stutthof (now Sztutowic) which lay to the north of Thorn near Danzig (now Gdansk). Originally a civilian internment camp Stutthof became a 'labour education' camp in 1941 under the control of the German Security Police. In January 1942 it became a regular concentration camp and by 1943 a crematorium, gas chamber and mobile gas wagons had been added ready to begin mass executions in June 1944 as part of the Final Solution.

Over the five years that Stalag XXA was in operation, over 60,000 prisoners of different nationalities passed through, including Poles, French, Belgians, Dutch, British, Russians, Yugoslavs, Italians, Norwegians, Americans.

British POWs were buried in the garrison military cemetery in Toruń, but their remains were later moved to the Commonwealth War Cemetery in Malbork, Poland.

Abbreviations and Place Names

BEF	British Expeditionary Force
FA	Field Ambulance
HD	Highland Division
ICRC	International Committee of the Red Cross
MI	Medical Inspection
MO	Medical Officer
NCO	Non-Commissioned Officer
NO	Nursing Orderly
POW	Prisoner of War
RAMC	Royal Army Medical Corps
TA	Territorial Army
152, 153, 154 FA	152nd, 153rd, 154th Field Ambulances

Place names during the German occupation of Poland and the present day

Danzig	Gdańsk
Graudenz	Grudiądz
Laskowitz	Laskowice
Marienburg	Malbork
Posen	Poznań
Stettin	Szczecin
Stutthof	Sztutowo
Thorn	Toruń

Names of fellow POWs noted in diaries

January- July 1940

MacRitchie, Enoch, Felmer, Martin, Carpenter, Young, Dey, Cameron, Morrison, Watkinson, Bunn, Cleghorn, Finlayson, Grimes, Elkins, Gover, Andrew, Kennedy, Woods, Smith, Philip, Tucker, Wright

August 1940 - October 1943

Graudenz: Alan Moore, Corporal Cook, Sergeant Akers, Major Duffus, Carter, Benny, Weeks, Butch

Thorn: Harry Morris, M Craig, Corporal Taylor, Maillie, Dodd, Miller, Taffy, Scottie, Corporal Ross, Maulcary, Jim Ross, Jack Watt, Ian Hay, Colonel Mackay, Murd

153 Fd Amb RAMC - Stalag XXA Internat 35 Graudenz

Lance Corporal Alistair C C MacRitchie, Private Allan Cameron, Private Archie M Dey, Private Alan Moore

Notes and References

There are many accounts of the fighting in France in 1940 and the events leading up to the capture of the 51st Highland Division. The most important ones we have drawn on for our narrative are: *Dunkirk-The men they left behind*, Sean Longden, Constable & Robinson Ltd, 2008; *The Highland Division*, Eric Linklater, HM Stationery Office, First Edition/Bloomsbury Reader 1942; *St Valery, The Impossible Odds*, Bill Innes, Birlinn Limited, 2004

CHAPTER TWO

1 *Inverness Courier,* 12 November 1918. With courtesy of Scottish Provincial Press. www.inverness-courier.co.uk/news/jubiliation-in-1918-as-the-great-war-is-over-139906/. Accessed 28 September 201.9

2 Inverness-shire RHA Regt 1/1st Battery
The 1/1st Inverness-shire Battery was based in the UK until February 1916 when they sailed to Alexandria in Egypt as part of the Egyptian Expeditionary Force (EEF). Here they were assigned to the ANZAC Mounted Division (Australian and New Zealand Mounted Division) as artillery support and fought in the Sinai and Palestine Campaign. Following the Battle of Romani in August 1916 the Division went on to join the Desert Column where William would have seen action from the Battle of Magdhaba (23 December 1916) through to the Second Battle of Gaza (17-19 April 1917).
http://www.scotlandswar.co.uk/inverness_rha.html
Accessed 25 June 2020.

3 *HMHS Llandovery Castle*
In June 1918 the ship became well-known when it was torpedoed by a German submarine off the coast of southern Ireland resulting in the deaths of 234 people. To try and cover up his action in firing at a hospital ship which was contrary to international law, the captain of the submarine ran down lifeboats and machine gunned many of the survivors. Twenty-four people on one remaining lifeboat survived. The sinking was one of the worst atrocities of the first world war and the case was presented at the Leipzig Trials.
https://www.ncbi.nlm.nih.gov/pmc/articles/PMC5973902/
Accessed 8 July 2019.

4 The Northern Barrage
Initially the partially assembled and specially designed sea mines were transported across the Atlantic to Kyle of Lochalsh on the west coast of Scotland. From here some were moved by train to Alness in Ross-shire. Others were moved by train and then barge up the Caledonian Canal to the Muirtown Basin in Inverness. Nearby distillery buildings at both locations were utilised and

huge sheds were constructed in which to complete the assembly of the sea mines ready for transportation to the mine layers out at sea.
https://www.facebook.com/InvernessLocalHistory/posts/world-war-one-part-5-base-18-america-in-invernessresearch-recent-photos-dave-con/1021142901361242/
Accessed 28 September 2019.

5   From the transcript of the Kings speech on the outbreak of World War Two, 3 September 1939.   Crown Copyright/OGL
https://www.historic-uk.com/HistoryUK/HistoryofBritain/The-Kings-Speech/. Article first published December 2014.
Accessed 18 August 2019.

6   Extract from British aerial propaganda leaflet dropped from aircraft over Germany. RAF, 3 and 4 September 1939. Over 6000 leaflets were dropped. *Inverness Courier,* 8 September 1939. With courtesy of Scottish Provincial Press.

CHAPTER FOUR

1   153rd Field Ambulance
According to the *RAMC Training Manual of 1935* a Field Ambulance (FA) was a mobile medical unit whose primary duty was 'to collect the sick and wounded and to arrange for their disposal'.
Royal Army Medical Corps Training 1935, HMSO, 1935. Pages 81, Item 177.

2   RAMC (Royal Army Medical Corps)
The Royal Army Medical Corps is a specialist corps in the British Army which provides medical services to all British Army personnel and their families in war and peace. Because it is not a fighting arm (non-combatant), under the Geneva Conventions, members of the RAMC are protected. During World War Two they were entitled to wear red cross armbands and also to display the emblem on their vehicles.
https://www.forces-war-records.co.uk/units/3307/royal-army-medical-corps
Accessed 8 July 2019.
Faithful in Adversity, The Royal Army Medical Corps in the Second World War, John Broom. Pen & Sword Military, 2019.

3   *The History of the 51st Highland Division 1939-1945,* J B Salmond. The Pentland Press Ltd, 1994.

4   *Inverness Courier,* 30 January 1940. With courtesy of Scottish Provincial Press.

5   *Inverness Courier,* 2 February 1940. With courtesy of Scottish Provincial Press.

6   *Royal Army Medical Corps Training 1935*, HMSO 1935. Page 81, Item 178. Page 87, Items 207 and 208.

7   *Inverness Courier,* 26 January 1940. With courtesy of Scottish Provincial Press.

8   The Maginot Line was an extensive series of fortifications built at great expense during the 1930s. It extended from the Swiss to the Franco-Belgian-Luxembourg borders and was intended to protect France's boundary with Germany. The Allies mistakenly believed it would provide a strong deterrent to the German army and prevent any large-scale attack.

    www.militaryhistorynow.com. Article 'The Maginot Line – 11 fascinating facts about France's great war', 7 May 2017. Accessed 20 April 2020.

9   *Inverness Courier*, 17 May 1940. With courtesy of Scottish Provincial Press.

10 *Christmas in the Lager – worse than a Sunday.* Compiled by Stuart MacRitchie, Blurb Inc., 2010.

CHAPTER SIX

1   *Inverness Courier*, 31 May 1940. With courtesy of Scottish Provincial Press (Extract from Ministry of Information announcement on evacuation of troops).

2   *Inverness Courier*, 31 May 1940. With courtesy of Scottish Provincial Press.

3   *Inverness Courier*, 31 May 1940. With courtesy of Scottish Provincial Press.

4   Extract from Major General Fortune's message, 11 June 1940. Crown Copyright/ OGL.
    The full text of this message can be found on:
    The War in France and Flanders 1939-40: A History of the Second World War, Major L F Ellis. Naval and Military Press, original publication 1953.
    www.ibiblio.org. Accessed 9 September 2019.

5   Extract from Major General Fortunes directive to the men, 11 June 1940. Crown Copyright/OGL.
    The full text of this directive can be found on:
    The War in France and Flanders 1939-40: A History of the Second World War, Major L F Ellis. Naval and Military Press, original publication 1953. www. ibiblio.org. Accessed 9 September 2019.

6   *Christmas in the Lager – worse than a Sunday.* Compiled by Stuart MacRitchie, Blurb Inc., 2010.

7   *Christmas in the Lager – worse than a Sunday.* Compiled by Stuart MacRitchie, Blurb Inc., 2010.

8   *Christmas in the Lager – worse than a Sunday.* Compiled by Stuart MacRitchie, Blurb Inc., 2010.

9   *Churchill's Sacrifice of the Highland Division, France 1940*, Saul David. Brassey's Military Books UK, 2004. Page 242. *The BEF in France, 1939-1940: Manning the Front through to the Dunkirk Evacuation,* Introduced and compiled by John Grehan & Martin Mace. Pen & Sword Military, 2014.

10 *Inverness Courier*, 14 June 1940. With courtesy of Scottish Provincial Press.

11   Extract from article entitled 'Highland Soldiers in Enemy Hands', *Inverness Courier*, 13 September 1940. With courtesy of Scottish Provincial Press.

12   Extract from Article 7 of *The Convention relative to the treatment of prisoners of war, Geneva July 27, 1929* or *The Geneva Convention*.www.icrc.org Accessed 2 February 2020.

13   *The Convention relative to the treatment of prisoners of war, Geneva July 27, 1929* or *The Geneva Convention*. www.icrc.org Accessed 29 July 2019. www.forces-war-records.co.uk/european-british-commonwealth-prisoners-of-war-1939-45 Accessed10 April 2020. https://ihl-databases.icrc.org/ihl/INTRO/305 accessed 21 September 2020.

14   *Christmas in the Lager – worse than a Sunday.* Compiled by Stuart MacRitchie, Blurb Inc., 2010.

15   From *United Nations War Crimes Commission Report* dated 16/6/1944. ©1944 United Nations. Reprinted with the permission of the United Nations.

16   *St Valery, The Impossible Odds*, Bill Innes, Birlinn Ltd, 2004. A Cameron Never Can Yield © Janette MacDonald. Translations and other material © Bill Innes. Reproduced with permission of The Licensor through PLSclear.

17   *Christmas in the Lager – worse than a Sunday.* Compiled by Stuart MacRitchie, Blurb Inc., 2010.

18   Albert Forster was appointed Gauleiter (Head) of the Reichsgau Danzig-West administration and their main objective was the total Germanisation of the Pomerania region within five years. In September 1939 a Gestapo murder squad was created called Einsatzkommando 16 and during the period from September to November 1939 across the region thousands of Jews, Poles and others were murdered by firing squads and buried in mass graves in the surrounding forests. Also involved in the de-Polonisation programme were members of the Volksdeutscher Selbstschutz (self-protection organisation). Comprised of German nationals living in Poland, these local groups assisted by rounding up Poles from surrounding towns and villages and holding them prisoner in old factory buildings, basements etc. The prisoners were brutally and often violently mistreated before most were earmarked for execution.

     The Pomeranian Crime 1939, Institute of National Remembrance, Commission for the Prosecution of Crimes Against the Polish Nation, Warsaw 2018.

19   Article 36, *The Convention relative to the treatment of prisoners of war, Geneva July 27, 1929* or *The Geneva Convention*. www.icrc.org Accessed 29 July 2019.

20   From the *Report of the International Committee of the Red Cross on its activities during the Second World War. Volume 1, May 1948.*

CHAPTER SEVEN

1   *The Telegraph*, 15 November 2011.

2   Extract from email received from a Junior Researcher, Antiques Roadshow, 13 January 2012.

CHAPTER EIGHT

1   Article 9 of *The Convention relative to the treatment of prisoners of war, Geneva July 27, 1929* or *The Geneva Convention*. www.icrc.org Accessed 2 February 2020.

2   *Report of the International Committee of the Red Cross on its activities during the Second World War, Volume 1, May 1948.*

3   Originally a civilian internment camp, Stutthof became a 'labour education' camp in 1941 under the control of the German Security Police. In January 1942 it became a regular concentration camp and by1943 a crematorium, gas chamber and mobile gas wagons had been added ready to begin mass executions in June 1944 as part of the Final Solution. https://www.forces-war-records.co.uk/european-camps-british-commonwealth-prisoners-of-war-1939-45. Accessed 1 July 2020.

4   Thesis: *Ukrainian Labourers in Nazi Germany in 1939-45*. Source: Library and Archives Canada/OCLC 681019904. https://bac-lac.on.worldcat.org/search?queryString=au%3DTelka%2C%20Stephen%20C&databaseList=283#/oclc/681019904. Accessed 21 February 2020.

5   Extract from *Inverness Courier*, 26 January 1940. Courtesy of Scottish Provincial Press.

6   Extract from *Inverness Courier*, 1 October 1940. Courtesy of Scottish Provincial Press.

7   *The Pomeranian Crime 1939*, Institute of National Remembrance, Commission for the Prosecution of Crimes Against the Polish Nation, Warsaw 2018.

8   Extract from Article 15 of T*he Convention relative to the treatment of prisoners of war, Geneva July 27, 1929*, or *The Geneva Convention*. www.icrc.org Accessed 2 February 2020.

9   From the *Report of the International Committee of the Red Cross on its activities during the Second World War. Volume 1, May 1948.*

10   From mid 1940 when thousands of POWs were captured, the ICRC increased their number of delegates. One of their most important tasks was to visit the POW camps to ensure that POWs treatment met the standards of the Geneva Convention. From the *Report of the International Committee of the Red Cross on its activities during the Second World War. Volume 1, May 1948.*

11 *The Pomeranian Crime 1939*, Institute of National Remembrance, Commission for the Prosecution of Crimes Against the Polish Nation, Warsaw 2018.

12 *Christmas in the Lager – worse than a Sunday*, compiled by Stuart MacRitchie. Blurb Inc., 2010.

13 *Christmas in the Lager – worse than a Sunday*, compiled by Stuart MacRitchie. Blurb Inc., 2010.

14 *Christmas in the Lager – worse than a Sunday*, compiled by Stuart MacRitchie. Blurb Inc., 2010.

15 Extract from Article 15 of *The Convention relative to the treatment of prisoners of war, Geneva July 27, 1929*, or *The Geneva Convention*. www.icrc.org Accessed 2 February 2020.

16 *Report of the International Committee of the Red Cross on its activities during the Second World War, Volume 1, May 1948*.

17 *Christmas in the Lager – worse than a Sunday*, compiled by Stuart MacRitchie. Blurb Inc., 2010.

18 Information supplied by Peter Duffus.

19 *Christmas in the Lager – worse than a Sunday*, compiled by Stuart MacRitchie. Blurb Inc., 2010.

20 *Christmas in the Lager – worse than a Sunday*, compiled by Stuart MacRitchie. Blurb Inc., 2010.

CHAPTER TEN

1 *Christmas in the Lager – worse than a Sunday*. Compiled by Stuart MacRitchie, Blurb Inc., 2010.

2 www.forces-war-records.co.uk/european-camps-british-commonwealth-prisoners-of-war-1939-45. Accessed July 2020.

3 Thesis: *Ukrainian Labourers in Nazi Germany 1939-45*
Source: Library and Archives Canada/OCLC 681019904
Accessed 21 April 2020.
https://bac-lac.on.worldcat.org/search?queryString=au%3DTelka%2C%20Stephen%20C&databaseList=283#/oclc/681019904

4 *The Barbed-Wire University, The Real Lives of Allied Prisoners of War in the Second World War*, Midge Gillies. Aurum Press Ltd, 2011.

5 Mail, censorship. http://www.caringonthehomefront.org.uk/search-the-library/writing-to-a-pow/. Accessed August 2017.

6 *Captives of War, British Prisoners of War in Europe in the Second World War*, Clare Makepeace. Cambridge University Press, 2017. Reproduced with

permission of The Licensor through PLSclear.

7   *The Prisoner of War* magazine, 18 May 1942 published by the Joint War Organisation of the British Red Cross and Order of St John.

8   From the *Report of the International Committee of the Red Cross on its activities during the Second World War, Volume 1, 1948.*

9   Article 17, *The Convention relative to the treatment of prisoners of war, Geneva July 27, 1929* or *The Geneva Convention.* www.icrc.org. Accessed 2 February 2020.

10   From the *Report of the International Committee of the Red Cross on its activities during the Second World War, Volume 1, 1948.*

11   Bodleian Libraries, 2013. Weston Library workers discover remnants of wartime book service. (Online). *https://www.bodleian.ox.ac.uk/bodley/news/2013,wartime-book-service.* Accessed 28 October 2020.

12   *The Prisoner of War* magazine, March 1943 published by the Joint War Organisation of the British Red Cross and Order of St John.

13   Obituary in *The Times* newspaper dated 10 September 1946. News Licensing, London. www.thetimes.co.uk. Accessed 15 April 2020.

CHAPTER ELEVEN

1   *The Guardian*, 1 March 2014. Courtesy of Guardian News & Media Ltd.

2   https://www.gedenkort-t4.eu/de/historische-orte/q5xnb-fort-vii-muzeum-martyrologii-wielkopolan. Accessed 4 February 2020.

3   https://www.thefirstnews.com/article/hitlers-first-death-camp-dubbed-fort-of-horror-opened-80-years-ago-today-in-poznan-8100. Accessed 27 October 2020.

4   Extract from Article 76, *The Convention relative to the treatment of prisoners of war, Geneva July 27, 1929* or The Geneva Convention. www.icrc.org Accessed 7 February 2020.

5   https://www.cwgc.org/find-a-cemetery/cemetery/2016901/malbork-commonwealth-war-cemetery/. Accessed 2 August 2019.

CHAPTER TWELVE

1   http://www.anzacpow.com/Part-5-Other-European-Free-Men/chapter_10_-_red_cross_repatriations. Accessed 5 July 2020.

2   http://www.anzacpow.com/Part-5-Other-European-Free-Men/chapter_10_-_red_cross_repatriations. Accessed 5 July 2020.

Footprints on the sands of time, Oliver Clutton-Brock. Grub Street Publishing, 2003. Online preview accessed 16 August 2019.

Christmas in the Lager – worse than a Sunday, compiled by Stuart MacRitchie, Blurb Inc., 2010.

3   www.victoriaharbour history.com/transportation/empress-of-russia. Accessed 16 August 2019.

4   *Footprints on the sands of time*, Oliver Clutton-Brock. Grub Street Publishing, 2003. Online preview accessed 16 August 2019.

5   Extract from the King's Message, *Inverness Courier*, 26 October 1943. Courtesy of Scottish Provincial Press.

6   Extract from letter men received whilst on board *Empress of Russia* reproduced in *Christmas in the Lager – worse than a Sunday*, compiled by Stuart MacRitchie. Blurb Inc., 2010.

7   Extract from *Inverness Courier*, 26 October 1943. Courtesy of Scottish Provincial Press.

8   Form regarding giving information to the enemy which men were required to sign. Extract from army questionnaire form reproduced in *Christmas in the Lager- worse than a Sunday*. Compiled by Stuart MacRitchie. Blurb Inc., 2010.

CHAPTER THIRTEEN

1   Extract from *Inverness Courier* article of 23 September 2014. Courtesy of Scottish Provincial Press.

2   Extract from *Inverness Courier* article of 23 September 2014. Courtesy of Scottish Provincial Press.

CHAPTER FOURTEEN

1   Courtesy of Lt Col Iain McIntyre.

Bibliography

Broom, John. *Faithful in Adversity, The Royal Army Medical Corps in the Second World War*. Pen & Sword Books Ltd, 2019.

Clutton-Brock, Oliver. *Footprints on the Sands of Time*. Grub Street Publishing, 2003.

David, Saul. *Churchill's Sacrifice of the Highland Division, France 1940*. Brassey's Books, October 2004.

Distante, Raphaël. *St Valery-en-Caux*. Editions Bénévent, 2005.

Doherty, Richard. *None Bolder, The History of the 51st Highland Division in the Second World War*. Spellmount Limited, 2006.

Gardner, Robert. *Kensington to St Valery-en-Caux, Princess Louise's Regiment, France and England, Summer 1940*. Spellmount, The History Press, 2012.

Gillies, Midge. *The Barbed-Wire University*. London: Aurum Press Limited, 2011.

Grehan, John, and Martin Mace. *The BEF in France, 1939-1940: Manning the Front through to the Dunkirk Evacuation*. Pen & Sword Military, 2014.

Grochowina, Sylwia, and Jan Sziling. *Barbarka. Miejsce Niemieckicj Egzekucji Polaków a Torunia I Okolic (Październik-Grudzién 1939)*. Fundacja Generał Zawackiej, 2009.

HMSO. *Royal Army Medical Corps Training 1935*. HMSO 1935.

Innes, Bill. *St Valery, The Impossible Odds*. Birlinn Limited, 2004.

Institute of National Remembrance, Commission for the Prosecution of Crimes Against the Polish Nation. *The Pomeranian Crime, 1939*. Warsaw, 2018.

Joint War Organisation of the British Red Cross and Order of St John. *The Prisoner of War* magazine, by the Joint War Organisation of the British Red Cross and Order of St John.

Linklater, Eric. *The Highland Division*. London: His Majesty's Stationery Office/ Bloomsbury Reader, 1942.

Longden, Sean. *Hitler's British Slaves, Allied POWs in Germany 1938-45*. Constable & Robinson, 2007.

Longden, Sean. *Dunkirk, The Men They Left Behind*. 2nd Edition, Constable & Robinson Ltd, 2008.

MacRitchie, Stuart. *Christmas in the Lager – worse than a Sunday*. Blurb Inc., 2010.

Makepeace, Clare. *Captives of War: British Prisoners of War in Europe in the Second*

World War. Cambridge: Cambridge University Press, 2017.

Mitchell, Stewart. *St Valery and its aftermath. The Gordon Highlanders captured in France in 1940*. Pen & Sword Books Limited, 2017.

Nicholls, T B. *Organisation, Strategy and Tactics of the Army Medical Services in War*. Bailliere, Tindall and Cox, 1937.

Salmond, J B. *The History of the 51st Highland Division 1939-1945*. Durham: 2nd Edition, The Pentland Press, 1994.

Websites

51hd. "51st Highland Division". Accessed July 2020. www.51hd.co.uk

British Red Cross. "Writing to a POW." Accessed August 2017. www.caringonthehomefront.org.uk/search-the-library/writing-to-a-pow/

Commonwealth War Graves Commission. "Malbork Commonwealth War Cemetery." Accessed 2 August 2019. www.cwgc.org/find-a-cemetery/cemetery/2016901/malbork-commonwealth-war-cemetery/

Doucet, J et al. "Massacre of Canadian Army Medical Corps personnel after the sinking of HMHS Llandovery Castle and the evolution of modern war crime jurisprudence." NCBI. Accessed 8 July 2019. www.ncbi.nlm.nih.gov/pmc/articles/PMC5973902/

Ellis, L F. The War in France and Flanders 1939-40: A History of the Second World War, Major L F Ellis. Naval and Military Press, original publication 1953. Accessed 9 September 2019. www.ibiblio.org.

Forces War Records. "Unit History: Royal Army Medical Corps." Forces War Records. Accessed July 2020. www.forces-war-records.co.uk/units/3307/royal-army-medical-corps

Forces War Records. "German Camps - British & Commonwealth Prisoners of War 1939-45." Accessed 10 April 2020. https://www.forces-war-records.co.uk/european-camps-british-commonwealth-prisoners-of-war-1939-45

Gedenkort -T4.eu. Fort VII Muzeum Martyrologii, Poznan. Accessed 4 February 2020. www.gedenkort-t4.eu/de/historische-orte/q5xnb-fort-vii-muzeum-martyrologii-wielkopolan

Historic UK. "King George VI." History of Britain. Accessed 18 August 2019. www.historic-uk.com/HistoryUK/HistoryofBritain/The-Kings-Speech/

Military History Now. "The Maginot Line – 11 fascinating facts about France's ill-fated fortifications", 7 May 2017. Accessed 20 April 2020. www.militaryhistorynow.com/2017/05/07/the-great-wall-of-france-11-remarkable-facts-about-the-maginot-line/

International Committee of the Red Cross. Report of the International Committee of the Red Cross on its activities during the Second World War, Volume 1. XVIIth International Red Cross Conference, Stockholm, August 1948. Accessed 2 February 2020. www.icrc.org.

International Committee of the Red Cross. "Convention relative to the Treatment of Prisoners of War, Geneva 1929." Treaties, States, Parties and Commentaries. Accessed 21 September 2020. https://ihl-databases.icrc.org/ihl/INTRO/305

Internet Archive. "The Northern Barrage, Mine Force, United States Atlantic Fleet, The North Sea 1918." Accessed 28 September 2019. www.archive.org/details/cu31924008602975/mode/2u

Inverness Local History Forum. 'World War One (Part 5) – Base 18 – America in Inverness." Accessed 28 September 2019. www.facebook.com/InvernessLocalHistory/posts/1021142901361242

Johnson, Ben. "The King's Speech." Historic UK, December 2014. Accessed 18 August 2019. www.historic-uk.com/HistoryUK/HistoryofBritain/The-Kings-Speech/

NCBI. "HMHS Llandovery Castle." Accessed 8 July 2019. www.ncbi.nlm.nih.gov/pmc/articles/PMC5973902/

Pendergast, Denton. "RMS Empress of Russia." Victoria Harbour History. accessed 16 August 2019. www.victoriaharbourhistory.com/transportation/empress-of-russia

Rudd, Bill. "Part 5, Chapter 10 -Red Cross Repatriation." Anzac POW freemen in Europe. Accessed 5 July 2020. www.anzacpow.com/Part-5-Other-Europhttps://51hd.co.ukean-Free-Men/chapter_10_-_red_cross_repatriations

Telka, Stephan C. Ukrainian Labourers in Nazi Germany, 1939-45. Carleton University Ottawa, Ontario, Canada, September 2008. Accessed 22 April https://bac-lac.on.worldcat.org/search?queryString=au%3DTelka%2C%20Stephen%20C&databaseList=283#/oclc/681019904

University of Edinburgh. "Inverness-shire Royal Horse Artillery." Scotland's War. Accessed 25 June 2020. www.scotlandswar.co.uk/inverness_rha.html